National Standards Curriculum Edition
Primary
Mathematics
for Jamaica

GRADE 6

Author
Raymond Simmonds and
Lillia Lewin-Robinson

Lead Advisor
Lorna Thompson

Series Editor
Paul Broadbent

HODDER
EDUCATION
AN HACHETTE UK COMPANY

The Publishers would like to thank the following for permission to reproduce copyright material.

Photo credits

Acknowledgements

Every effort has been made to trace all copyright holders, but if any have been inadvertently overlooked, the Publishers will be pleased to make the necessary arrangements at the first opportunity.

Although every effort has been made to ensure that website addresses are correct at time of going to press, Hodder Education cannot be held responsible for the content of any website mentioned in this book. It is sometimes possible to find a relocated web page by typing in the address of the home page for a website in the URL window of your browser.

Hachette UK's policy is to use papers that are natural, renewable and recyclable products and made from wood grown in sustainable forests. The logging and manufacturing processes are expected to conform to the environmental regulations of the country of origin.

Orders: please contact Bookpoint Ltd, 130 Park Drive, Milton Park, Abingdon, Oxon OX14 4SE. Telephone: (44) 01235 827720. Fax: (44) 01235 400454. Email education@bookpoint.co.uk. Lines are open from 9 a.m. to 5 p.m., Monday to Saturday, with a 24-hour message answering service. You can also order through our website: www.hoddereducation.com

ISBN: 978 1 5104 0057 3

First published in 2018
Second edition published in [date]
This edition published in 2018 by
Hodder Education,
An Hachette UK Company
Carmelite House
50 Victoria Embankment
London EC4Y 0DZ

www.hoddereducation.com

Impression number   10 9 8 7 6 5 4 3 2 1
Year   2022 2021 2020 2019 2018

Illustrations by Oxford Designs and Illustrators Ltd.
Typeset in India by Aptara Inc.
Printed in TK

A catalogue record for this title is available from the British Library.

Contents

Term 3

Using this book

For the Students

Mathematics is all around us, with important skills and knowledge that you will use in your everyday life. It is also an amazing and interesting subject for you to enjoy. This textbook will help you master the different areas of mathematics, with activities and exercises to support your learning and give you practice.

Most importantly, the book will also encourage you to **think** like a mathematician! There are lots of problem-solving activities that will challenge you. This is great as you should be asking questions as well as answering them and spending time exploring the mathematics.

Mathematics is creative, so make sure you look for patterns, investigate and talk about the activities. It is also good to work together and support each other to solve problems.

We hope you enjoy working with this course!

- Your teacher will use the **Explain** boxes to help your understanding, so read these carefully and work through the examples.

- The **Remember** boxes are small reminders to give you advice and jog your memory.

- **Try this** activities will extend the mathematics or use it in a different way

- The **Reasoning** activities will need you to think carefully and explain what you are doing and why you are doing it. These may not all have a single answer, so explore, work with others and be creative.

For the Teachers

This mathematics series is intended to be used as a teaching and learning tool to support you with your planning and teaching and to give your students a rich variety of activities to help them master skills, concepts and procedures. It has been written and revised by Jamaican educators in line with Jamaica's National Standards Curriculum (NSC), with the structure and format of the series aiming to develop a depth of understanding through its careful progression.

The approach is in-line with current thinking on the teaching of mathematics, with an emphasis on the 21st Century Skills of critical thinking, creativity, collaboration and communication.

Critical thinking
Opportunities for reasoning, problem-solving and strategic thinking are essential in helping students develop a depth of understanding of mathematical ideas and concepts. Reasoning activities shown by the <> logo encourage critical thinking, with problems to solve and questions that ask students to show their reasoning and explain their results.

Creativity
Mathematics is a creative subject and, wherever appropriate, this series includes opportunities to explore, build, investigate, design and link to other areas of the curriculum. References and examples are also reflective of the Jamaican experience to show mathematics used in everyday situations.

Collaboration
Pairs or small groups of students are encouraged to collaborate to help each other solve the problems in the **Try this** and **Reasoning** activities. There are also opportunities to work together as a class through the **Explain** activities, discussing the examples and explanation shown.

Communication
Students can explain what they are doing and why they are doing it, through probing questioning. Questions should allow students to talk, explain and show their understanding and reasoning, for example: '*What do you notice?*', '*Can you see a pattern?*', '*What have you discovered?*', '*How did you find that out?*', '*Why do you think that?*', '*Can you explain your reasoning?*'

The wide range of activities within the textbooks also reflect **Webb's Depth of Knowledge** model. The 4 DOK levels are not sequential or developmental, but it is important that students have a broad experience of all the levels to gain a deep understanding of the mathematics:

DOK-1 Recall and reproduction
DOK-2 Basic application of skills and concepts
DOK-3 Strategic thinking
DOK-4 Extended thinking

The activities shown by the <> **logo** have a particular Level 3 focus and require reasoning and higher order thinking skills than Level 1 and 2 activities. There are also **Extended Projects** each term that give opportunities for Level 4 extended thinking.

Formative assessment is an important part of teaching and learning, checking that students have a good understanding of concepts and skills before moving on with the learning. **Assess and Review** questions are also provided in the textbooks to give teachers the opportunity to evaluate the progress of the students.

1 Sets

Members of sets

Explain

A **set** is a well-defined collection of items.
Here is an example:
If V is the set of vowels, this set is written as   V = {a, e, i, o, u}
Set V has five members or **elements**.
We use the sign ∈ to show that an item is a member or element of the set.
For example: a ∈ {a, e, i, o, u}.
We can use the sign ∉ to show that an item is not a member of a set.
For example: b ∉ {a, e, i, o, u}.
A set that has no elements is called an **empty set**.
The symbol for an empty set is ∅ or { }.

V = (a e i o u)

1 Using curly brackets, list the members of these sets.

   a five subjects you study   **b** three animals that can swim

   c letters in your name

2 How many members are there in the following sets?

   a odd numbers between 0 and 10   **b** days of the week

   c even numbers between 5 and 15   **d** whole numbers between 6 and 7

3 Copy these and fill in the missing words or symbols.
   _____ or _____ is the symbol for an empty set. An empty set has _____ members.

4 John was given these items to make sets.

   He made sets A and B.

   What do you notice about the sets?

5 Show how you can make sets from these items.

6 Copy these and fill in the missing symbol ∈ or ∉.

   a

   b y ○ {a, e, i, o, u}

   c 3 ○ {whole numbers between 1 and 10}   **d** 1 ○ {even numbers}

   e p ○ {letters in my name}   **f** Monday ○ {days of the week}

Equivalent sets

Equivalent sets have the same number of elements.

The elements do not have to be the same.

This symbol shows equivalent sets: ⟷

This symbol shows that sets are not equivalent: ⟷̸

For example: {🌴, ✳, ●} ⟷ {A, B, C}

{✳, △, ■} ⟷̸ {Q, R, S, T}

1 The sets in column B have been scrambled. Match each set in column A with an equivalent set in column B. For example:

{🌧, 🌧, ⚡, ⛈, 🌬} and {Monday, Tuesday, Wednesday, Thursday, Friday}

Column A	Column B
A { 🐱, 🐱, 🐱, 🐱, 🐱, 🐱 }	a {1, 0}
B { 🐄, 🐐, 🐖 }	b {□, ○, △, ◇, □}
C { 🏠, ⛪ }	c {1/2, 3/4, 7/8, 9/10, 5/5, 4/7}
D { 🎾, 🥎, 🏀, 🏐 }	d {27, 28, 29, 30}
E { 🧢, 🎩, 👒, 👒, 👨‍🍳 }	e {x, y, z}

2 Draw four examples of equivalent sets with six elements.

3 Copy these and fill in the symbol ⟷ or ⟷̸ between each pair of sets.

a {6, 3, 2, 1} ○ {△, ○, □, ⬠, ☆}

b {🌴, 🌴, 🌴} ○ {C, +, ÷}

c {=, >, √, π} ○ {1/2, 1/3, 3/4, 3/7}

d {A, B, C} ○ {?, !, ;}

e { 🧒🧒🧒🧒🧒 } ○ { 🧒🧒🧒🧒🧒 }

f {factors of 9} ○ {factors of 8}

Remember

Equivalent sets have equal numbers of elements, even if the elements are not the same.

Finite and infinite sets

Any set with limited members is a **finite set**.

For example: Set Y = {dogs, cats, rats}

                 Set Y has only three members so it is limited.

Any set with unlimited members is an **infinite set**.

For example, we can express the set of counting numbers as   C = {1, 2, 3, 4, …}

The … means that the set continues to infinity.

The set of counting numbers goes on forever, as we can keep adding 1 to each number to get to another, bigger, number. A set that goes on forever and cannot be counted is called an **infinite set**.

1 Write **finite set** or **infinite set** for each of these sets.

    a months of the year   **b** factors of 7   **c** multiples of 7

    d seconds in one minute   **e** stars in the sky   **f** letters of the alphabet

2 Describe each set and say whether it is finite or infinite.

    a {0, 1, 2, 3, … 18, 19, 20}   **b** {2, 4, 6, 8, 10, …}   **c** {1, 2, 5, 10}

    d {50, 100, 150, … 450, 500}   **e** {1, 3, 5, 7, …}

3 Represent each of the following sets using set notation.

    a the set of multiples of 5

    b the set of even numbers

    c the set of odd numbers between 1 and 20

    d the set of factors of 100

    e the set of days of the week

    f the set of months that have 30 days

Try this

Using the information on this page, explain what *infinity* means to your classmate.

As a quick research activity, use the Internet to find out how many stars there are in the universe. Is the universe finite or infinite?

Reasoning activity

Are these statements always true, sometimes true or never true? Explain your reasoning. How could you prove you are right?

a A finite set may be a member of an infinite set.

b An infinite set may be a member of a finite set.

c It is possible for a set to be both finite and infinite.

Subsets

Explain

⊂ means 'is a subset of'. ⊄ means 'is not a subset of'.

This is Gina's family: {Nathan, Amelia, Jamie, Rebecca, Arthur, Jimmy, Gina, Dolly}

{Jimmy, Gina, Jamie} ⊂ {Nathan, Amelia, Jamie, Rebecca, Arthur, Jimmy, Gina, Dolly}

This means that the set of the children is a subset of Gina's family.

1 Say whether each statement is true or false.

   a {Jupiter, Neptune} ⊂ {planets of the Solar System}

   b 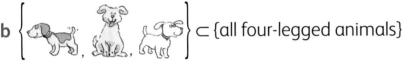 ⊂ {all four-legged animals}

   c 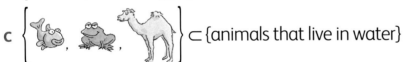 ⊂ {animals that live in water}

   d {Trinidad, St Lucia, Barbados} ⊂ {Caribbean islands}

   e {Monday, Tuesday} ⊂ {months of the year}

2 List three of the subsets of the set {1, 2, 3, 4}.

3 Make four subsets of polygons.

4 a List five members of the set of sports.

   b List four subsets of the set of sports.

5 Write down how many members are in each of the following sets and list one subset of each set.

   a days of the week   b months of the year

   c planets in the Solar System   d students in your class

Disjoint sets

A = {▲, ■, ●}
B = {1, 2, 3}
Set A and set B are equivalent sets, because they have the same number of elements.
However, they have no common elements. When two sets have no common elements, they are called **disjoint** sets.

1 Look at the diagrams and answer the questions that follow.

Figure 1

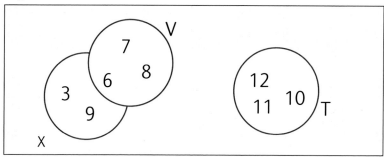

Figure 2

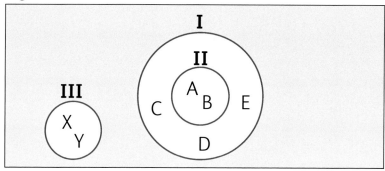

   a Name the disjoint set in Figure 1.
   b Name the disjoint sets in Figure 2.
   c Why are sets V and X not disjoint sets?
   d Why are sets II and III in Figure 2 disjoint sets?

Remember

Disjoint sets are two sets that share no elements at all. In a Venn diagram, they are represented as separate circles with no overlaps.

Reasoning activity

Draw a diagram to show set A of the primary colours (red, yellow and blue), and set B of the secondary colours (orange, green and purple). What is the relationship between the two sets?

Intersecting sets and union of sets

Explain

The **intersection** of two sets is the set of elements common to both sets.
The symbol for intersection is ∩.
For example:
{■, △, ⬤, ★, ◆} ∩ {■, ★, ❁} = {■, ★}

1 Copy and complete these.

  a {1, 2, 3, 4, 5, 6} ∩ {2, 4, 6, 8, 10} =

  b {1, 2, 4, 7, 11, 16, 21} ∩ {whole numbers from 0 to 15} =

  c {a, b, c, d, e, f, g} ∩ {b, e, i, v, w} =

  d {even numbers between 3 and 11} ∩ {prime numbers between 1 and 10} =

Explain

The **union** of two sets is the set of all the elements contained in either of them.
We do not write any elements twice. The symbol for union is ∪.
For example:
{Romy, Gina, Michael, Andrew, Steve} ∪ {Romy, Steve, Danny, Andrea}
  = {Romy, Gina, Michael, Andrew, Steve, Danny, Andrea}
{■, ▲, ⬤, ◣} ∪ {◆, ◣, ★, ⬤} = {■, ▲, ⬤, ◣, ◆, ★}

2 Copy and complete these.

  a {Harry, Angie, Tina} ∪ {Angie, Sally, Farouk, Nina, Tina} =

  b {50, 60, 70, 80, 90, 100} ∪ {95, 90, 85, 80} =

  c {1, 4, 9, 16, 25} ∪ {4, 8, 10, 12, 14, 16} =

3 Copy these and fill in ∪ or ∩ in each circle.

  a {2, 3, 4} ◯ {1, 2, 3, 4, 5, 6} = {2, 3, 4}

  b {days of the week} ◯ {days of the weekend}
      = {Monday, Tuesday, Wednesday, Thursday, Friday, Saturday, Sunday}

  c { 🍈, 🍌, 🥭, 🍇, 🍐 } ◯ { 🍊, 🍐, 🍈, 🍎, 🍌 } = { 🍊, 🍈, 🍌 }

  d {0.002, 0.001, 0.022, 0.011, 0.222} ◯ {0.02, 0.022, 0.012, 0.222, 0.01}
      = {0.022, 0.222}

Venn diagrams

This is a **Venn diagram**. The set of letters of the alphabet is a universal set. That means it is the main set of elements we are talking about. The set of vowels is a subset of the universal set.

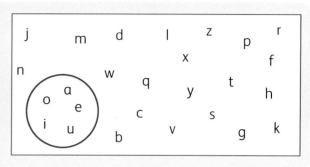

1 Draw Venn diagrams to show the following:

	Universal set	Subset
a	numbers from 1 to 10	prime numbers
b	odd numbers between 2 and 20	composite numbers
c	numbers from 1 to 20	factors of 24
d	prime numbers between 5 and 50	13, 17, 23
e	multiples of 10 between 1 and 99	multiples of 20

2 Copy and complete the Venn diagrams to show the given subsets.

a
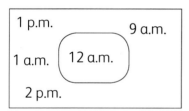

{midnight, midday} ⊂ {hours of the day}

b
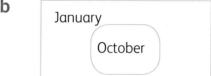

{last three months} ⊂ {months of the year}

c

{blue, yellow, green} ⊂ {colours of the rainbow}

d
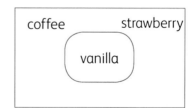

{vanilla, chocolate} ⊂ {ice-cream flavours}

3 Copy and complete the following Venn diagrams.

a {whole numbers from 1 to 15}

b {letters of the alphabet}

More Venn diagrams

Use the Venn diagram below to answer the questions that follow.

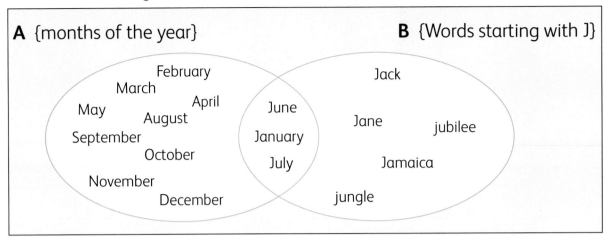

A {months of the year}   **B** {Words starting with J}

February
March
April
May
August
September
October
November
December
June
January
July
Jack
Jane
jubilee
Jamaica
jungle

1 a Use set notation to write the intersection of sets A and B.

b Name some other elements of set B not shown in the diagram above.

c Would your name be an element of set A or set B or neither?
Give a reason for your answer.

2 Set C is the set of words that end in the letter 'r'.

a List the elements of set A that would intersect with set C.

b Think of some elements that would be in the intersection of sets B and C.

3 Write the union and intersection of the sets shown in these Venn diagrams.

a
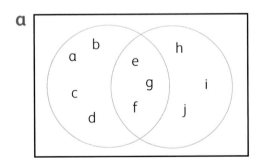

b
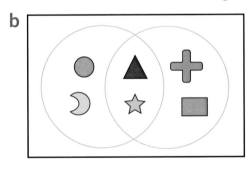

Remember

A Venn diagram is a simple diagram in which all the elements are drawn or written and circled by a ring or other closed shape that marks out which elements are contained within the set.

2 Number

Hindu-Arabic number system

Reasoning activity

Play a game of **Making numbers** in pairs.
You will need: digit cards 0–9.
Shuffle the cards and

| 0 | 1 | 2 | 3 | 4 | 5 | 6 | 7 | 8 | 9 |

place them face down on the table.
Take turns to play. The aim is to make the largest possible number with five selected digits.
Player 1 selects one digit card at a time and places it in one of these five squares. Once a card is placed, it cannot be moved.
Once the 5-digit number is complete, check it.
If it is the largest possible number, player 1 wins 1 point.
Player 2 has their turn, selecting and placing five digit cards.
Play continues until one player has won 5 points.
Play the game again, this time trying to make the smallest possible number.

Talk about

Discuss in pairs.
How many digits are there in the Hindu-Arabic number system?
Are there any other number systems that you know?

Explain

Talk about the game.
What can you say about the digits in the first square?
What about the last square?
A **place value chart** helps us to identify the place value and true value of a digit in a number.

Millions	Hundred thousands	Ten thousands	Thousands	Hundreds	Tens	Ones
6	3	9	7	4	3	2

The digit 9 has a true value of 90 000 and a place value of ten thousands.

1 Write the true value and the place value of each red digit in this number.

4 6 **9** 2 1 8 7 5

		True value	Place value
a	4		
b	6		
c	2		
d	8		

Working with numbers

The table shows how many slabs of chocolate were sold by eight supermarkets during one month.

1 Which supermarket made sales of six hundred thousand and one slabs?

2 Which supermarket made the most sales?

3 Write in words how many slabs were sold by:

a Dennis & Co   b Everything Shop

c Grocery Garden   d Hunter & Son.

4 These are the numbers of boxes of bananas and boxes of oranges sent to four countries. Copy the table, writing the numbers in figures instead of words.

Supermarket	Number of slabs sold
Appleton Store	1 460 305
Brown's Bargains	30 700
Chain Store	9 407 518
Dennis & Co	300 924
Everything Shop	8 946 503
Fresh Food Store	600 001
Grocery Garden	16 305
Hunter & Son	6 000 001

Country	Boxes of bananas	Boxes of oranges
Canada	three million, five hundred thousand and fifty	three million and nine
United Kingdom	two million, seven hundred and sixty thousand, three hundred and twenty-five	nine hundred and twenty-seven thousand, six hundred and fifty
USA	four million, five hundred and eighty	one and a half million
Germany	three-quarters of a million	one and a quarter million

5 Copy the table and fill in the value of the underlined digits. The first one has been done for you.

	Number	Value of digit
a	41**5**6	5 tens = 50
b	15**2** 309	
c	1 800 00**7**	
d	2 4**1**9 024	
e	**8**52 600	
f	3 **9**36	

6 Write 4 different numbers for each of these that have:

a five digits, with a 3 in the tens place

b four digits, with a 9 in the thousands place

c six digits, with a 2 in the hundred thousands place

d seven digits, with a 4 in the millions place.

Large numbers in real life

1 Compare the salaries of these people.

| Mr John | Mr Binks | Ms Byer | Ms Brown | Ms Smith |

$120 944.00 $96 780.00 $49 440.00 $8100.00 $4800.00

   a Who earns the highest salary?

   b Who earns the lowest salary?

   c Write the salaries in order, starting with the lowest.

2 The table shows the populations of some small countries.

   a Which country has the largest population?

   b Which country has a population of almost 1 million people?

   c Which countries have populations of more than 1 million people?

   d Which countries have populations of fewer than half a million people?

   e Write the populations of these countries in words:

      a Norway   b Barbuda   c Barbados

   f Write the populations of these countries in expanded notation:

      a Kuwait   b Swaziland   c Belize

Country	Population
Norway	4 247 546
Barbuda	1 400
Barbados	269 000
Mauritius	1 180 000
Belize	242 000
Kuwait	1 970 000
Swaziland	984 000

Talk about

Where do we use large numbers in real life? What is the largest number you have heard of or used?

Powers of 10

Explain

The highest mountain in Jamaica, the Blue Mountain, is 2 256 metres above sea level. We can write this number in different ways:

Numeral   2 256
Word form   Two thousand two hundred and fifty-six
Expanded form   2000 + 200 + 50 + 6
Exponential form $(2 \times 10^3) + (2 \times 10^2) + (5 \times 10^1) + (6 \times 10^0)$

1 Write these numbers in word, expanded and exponential forms.
    a 67 389   b 305 421   c 9 562 834   d 4 007 992

2 Write these as numerals.
    a $(2 \times 10^6) + (3 \times 10^5) + (4 \times 10^2) + (4 \times 10^1) + (3 \times 10^0)$
    b $(7 \times 10^5) + (2 \times 10^4) + (3 \times 10^3) + (2 \times 10^0)$
    c $(2 \times 10^6) + (4 \times 10^2) + (1 \times 10^0)$
    d $(4 \times 10^0) + (7 \times 10^5) + (4 \times 10^3) + (7 \times 10^2)$

Explain

$10 \times 10 = 100$
10×10 can be written as 10^2 We say 'ten squared' or 'ten to the power 2'
$10 \times 10 \times 10 = 1000$ or 10^3 We say 'ten cubed' or 'ten to the power 3'
$10 \times 10 \times 10 \times 10 = 10^4$ ten to the power 4
$10 \times 10 \times 10 \times 10 \times 10 = 10^5$ ten to the power 5

A number written as powers like this uses an **exponent**. In 8^2 the number 8 is the base and the 2 is the exponent. An exponent tells us how many times the base is multiplied by itself. When you multiply powers with the same base, you can add exponents.
$10^3 \times 10^2 = 10 \times 10 \times 10 \times 10 \times 10 = 10^5$ $(10^3 \times 10^2 = 10^{3+2} = 10^5)$

3 Work out the value of:
    a 10^3 b 2^3 c 1^3 d 2^4 e 10^4

4 Work out these.
    a $10^2 \times 10^2$ b $10^3 \times 10^4$
    c $10^2 \times 10^4$

5 Work out the value of:
    a 10 to the power 6
    b 2 to the power 5

Reasoning activity

Work out the difference between these. Explain your working.
a $(10^4 \times 10^1)$ and 10^6
b 2 to the power 4 and 2 to the power 1

Decimals

Explain

The decimal system is a place value system with base 10. The base is the same as the number of single-digit numbers in a number system. Our number system has ten single digits (0 to 9). We use a decimal point to show the change in place value from whole numbers to fractions.

100s	10s	1s	.	10ths	100ths	1000ths	10 000ths
4	1	6	.	2	0	5	8

The value of the 2 in the example above is $\frac{2}{10}$, two tenths or 0.2.

The value of the 5 in the example above is $\frac{5}{1000}$, five thousandths or 0.005.

The value of the 8 in the example above is $\frac{8}{10000}$, eight ten-thousandths or 0.0008.

1 Write these numbers using decimals.

   a one and four-tenths

   b nine and thirteen-hundredths

   c three and four-thousandths

   d eight point seven two nine

   e one point zero zero five

   f eighteen point zero eight one

2 Find the value of the 5 in each of the following decimals.

   Write your answer as a fraction and as a decimal.

   a 0.058   b 49.529   c 98.775   d 144.56   e 22.4415

3 Copy the table and write the value of the circled digit in words and as a fraction.

Decimal	Value in words	Value as a fraction
0.5612	six hundredths	$\frac{6}{100}$
55.967188		
0.00012		
90 000.1005		
150.99		
187.0530		
1 762.3128		

Talk about

Decimals are found in many places in our daily lives, for example in prices, on petrol pump gauges, on car odometers and in sports times. Work in pairs to make a list of at least ten other examples of decimals in our daily lives.

Rounding and ordering decimals

1 Round these to the nearest whole number.

   a 805.6   b 6 095.1   c 2.8   d 300.9   e 674.3   f 8 105.7

2 Round these to the nearest tenth.

   a 342.82   b 609.172   c 65.519   d 819.086   e 80.043   f 403.28

3 Round these to the nearest hundredth.

   a 1.10044   b 5.0525   c 9.0189   d 2.306   e 1.1119   f 177.1979

4 Round these to the nearest thousandth.

   a 55.97188   b 176.01429   c 4 000.6758   d 19 056.33888

Talk about

Look at the picture and discuss it in pairs. Is the man correct? Why or why not?

Why do people round their height, age or weight?

With a friend, make a list of three situations when you need to find an accurate measurement and three situations when a rounded measurement will be accurate enough.

5 The drawing shows you the heights of trees in a botanical garden. Use the letters to list the trees in order from tallest to shortest.

6 Write each set of decimals in order of size, starting with the smallest.

   a 1.98, 0.198, 0.00198, 19.8, 0.981, 0.00189

   b 6.77, 7.77, 7.78, 9.11, 1.99, 0.177

   c 0.01, 0.002, 0.011, 0.0011, 0.0009

   d 7.651, 7.179, 1.999, 2.708, 6.5091

Estimating and using calculators

Explain

You can use rounding to help you estimate the answers to mathematics problems. When you use a calculator, the answer is sometimes a long decimal. You can also use rounding to shorten these long numbers. When we use rounding, we find an **approximate** answer.

We use the ≈ sign, which means 'almost equal to'.

46.3 ÷ 5.8   First round each number to the nearest whole number.

46.3 ≈ 46 and 5.8 ≈ 6   So the calculation becomes 46 ÷ 6

46 is not a multiple of 6. The nearest multiple of 6 is 48.

48 ÷ 6 = 8   So 46 ÷ 6 ≈ 8

Now check your answer using a calculator, and compare it with your estimate.

4 6 . 3 ÷ 5 . 8 =   7.982758621

Round the calculator's answer to the nearest whole number.

46.3 ÷ 5.8 ≈ 8

---

1 Estimate the answer to each calculation by rounding to the nearest whole number and working out an approximate answer.

   a 57.6 ÷ 4.3   b 72.4 ÷ 8.5   c 24.9 ÷ 6.2   d 109.3 ÷ 11.8

   e 624.7 ÷ 5.3   f 3 658.3 ÷ 23.8   g 1 945.1 ÷ 4.8   h 199.82 ÷ 9.9

   i 227.9 ÷ 2.7   j 713.7 ÷ 6.6

2 Now use your calculator to check your answers. Round the calculator answer to the nearest whole number and compare it with the estimate from Question 1.

Try this

Key in the number 77345 on your calculator.
Now turn the calculator upside down. What word have you spelled?
Work out what number you must key in to spell the following words.

a SOIL   **b** SHOE   **c** LOSS   **d** LEE   **e** SEE

3 Problems and patterns

Story problems using operations

Price list	
Item	**Price ($)**
1 tin milk	155.00
1 kg rice	56.00
1 kg brown sugar	40.00
1 kg flour	28.00
500 ml cooking oil	76.00

1   Use this price list to solve these problems.

   a   George goes to the shop to buy 4 tins of milk, 3 kilograms of rice, 2 kilograms of sugar and 1 kilogram of flour.

   How much money does he spend altogether?

   b   He pays with $1000.00. How much change does he get?

   c   Tanya has $500.00. How many tins of milk can she buy?

   d   Sally buys 5 kilograms of sugar and Michael buys 5 kilograms of rice. Work out the difference between the totals that they spend.

   e   Peter buys 6 litres of cooking oil and 8 kilograms of rice. On which item did he spend more money?

   f   Andrew has $900.00.
   These are the items he needs to buy:

   How much more money does he need to buy all the items on his list?

9 kilograms of sugar
6 tins of milk
10 kilograms of rice

Reasoning activity

   a   Find a supermarket advertisement from a local newspaper. Choose six items from the advertisement. Write the name of each item and its price.

   b   Make up five story problems about the items you have chosen.

   c   Exchange story problems with a classmate and solve each other's story problems.

Number patterns

A **sequence** is a list of numbers that follow a pattern.

1 Try to describe the patterns shown on these number lines.

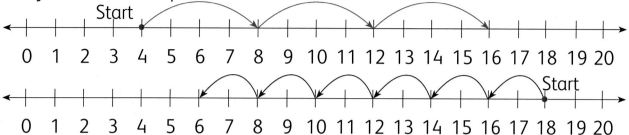

2 Copy and complete these sequences.
   For each sequence, explain the pattern.

   a 5, 9, 13, 17, ___ , ___ , ___

   b 29, 27, 25, ___ , ___ , ___

   c 4, 12, 36, ___ , ___ , ___

   d 3 125, 625, 125, ___ , ___ , ___

   e 5, 15, 45, ___ , ___ , ___

   f 2, 5, 11, 23, ___ , ___ , ___

Reasoning activity

This pizza must be shared between a crowd of friends.
When the pizza is cut straight across the middle, it is divided into two pieces.
When it is cut a second time, it is divided into four pieces.

Copy and complete the table.

Number of cuts	1	2	3	4	5	6	7	8
Pieces of pizza	2	4						

a What is the pattern in the first sequence (number of cuts)?

b What is the pattern in the second sequence (pieces of pizza)?

c How many times would you cut the pizza to have enough pieces for everyone in your classroom?

d How big or small do you think the slices would be? Why?

Number sequences

Explain

Look at this sequence: 4, 8, 12, 16, 20, ...

What would be the value of the nth term in the sequence?

Position in sequence	1	2	3	4	5	6	n
Term	4	8	12	16	20	24	$n \times 4$

We can describe this sequence in different ways:

- Add 4 to the previous term.
- Multiply the position of the term in the sequence by 4.
- If t is the term and n is the position of the term, $t = n \times 4$.

1 Copy and complete each table with the missing terms.

a

Position in sequence (n)	1	2	3	4	5	6	n
Term (t)	5	10	15		25		

b

Position in sequence (n)	1	2	3	4	5	6	n
Term (t)	0	7	14	21			

c

Position in sequence (n)	1	2	3	4	5	6	n
Term (t)	100	99	98	97	96		

2 For each table in Question 1, write an algebraic expression using t and n.

3 Write the first ten terms in each sequence, where n is the position of the term in the sequence and t is the term.

  a $t = 3 \times n$ **b** $t = 15 \times n$

  c $t = n + 25$ **d** $t = (n \times 5) + 1$

  e $t = (n \times 3) + 10$

4 In your own words, describe the rule that generates each sequence.

  a 1, 3, 5, 7, 9, 11, ...   **b** 1, 2, 4, 7, 11, 16, ...

  c 1, 4, 9, 16, 25, ...   **d** 10, 100, 1 000, 10000, ...

  e 1, 8, 27, 64, ...

 **Scale**

Units of measurement

Explain

Metric unit of length	kilometre	metre	centimetre	millimetre
Abbreviation	km	m	cm	mm

1 What is the most appropriate unit for measuring the length of each item?

a   b   c  d   e

f 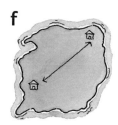 g 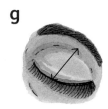 h 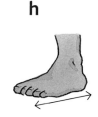 i

2 Measure the length of these, first to the nearest centimetre, and then in millimetres.

a  b

c d

3 Estimate each of these. Compare your estimations with those of a friend.

   a the length of your longest finger **b** the height of your classroom

   c the distance from school to the nearest airport **d** the height of the tallest tree in your street

4 Measure these lines in centimetres. Write your answers as decimals.

   a _____ b _____

   c _____ d _____

Talk about

If 1 cm represents 500 metres, what distance does each line in Question 4 represent?

Scale measurements

Talk about

Look at these photographs.

a Measure the height of the object in each photograph.
Write the height of each object in centimetres.

b Is this the actual height of these objects?
Explain why they appear much smaller in the photographs than they really are.

Explain

When something is drawn smaller than it really is, but in the same proportion, we say it has been drawn to **scale**. The scale of a map tells us the size on the map compared with the real size. For example, a scale of 1:5 means the map or drawing is $\frac{1}{5}$ of the size of the real thing. In other words, 1 unit measured on the map represents 5 of the same units in reality.

Look at this map showing two villages.
Use it find the answers to these questions.

1 How far is it from A to B on the map?

2 1 cm on the map represents 1 km in reality.
How far is it from A to B in reality?

3 What is the real distance between:

  a A and G   **b** A and F?

4 Mrs Brown walked from C to D and over the bridge to E.
Approximately how far did she walk altogether in kilometres?

5 A bus makes four trips between the bus stops in the villages each day.

  a What is the distance between the two bus stops in kilometres?

  b How far does the bus travel in a day?

  c What distance does the bus driver cover between the villages in a week (7 days)?

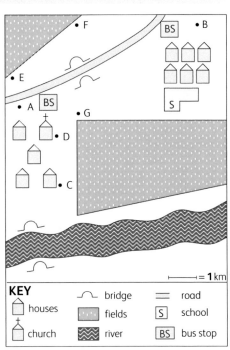

KEY

🏠	houses	bridge	road
⛪	church	fields	S school
		river	BS bus stop

Finding distances on maps

The names of some countries are shown
on this map of South America.
The capital cities of these countries
are shown by a dot.

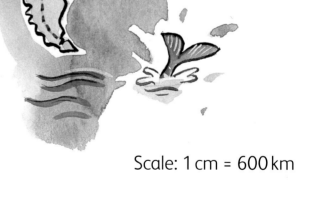

1 What is the scale of this map?
What does this tell you?

2 Measure these distances on the map.
Write your answers in centimetres.

   a from Caracas to Brasilia

   b from Brasilia to La Paz

   c from La Paz to Caracas

3 Calculate the real distances between
the cities in Question 2 in kilometres.

4 How wide is South America at its widest
point? Measure this in centimetres and
then calculate the real distance.

Scale: 1 cm = 600 km

5 Approximately how many kilometres
is it from Caracas to the southern tip of
South America?

Remember

To calculate the real-life distances shown on
the map, you will need to multiply by 600 and
express the units as km.

Scale drawings

On this map, 1 cm represents 100 metres, which is 10 000 cm.
Use your ruler to measure the distances for Questions 1 and 2.

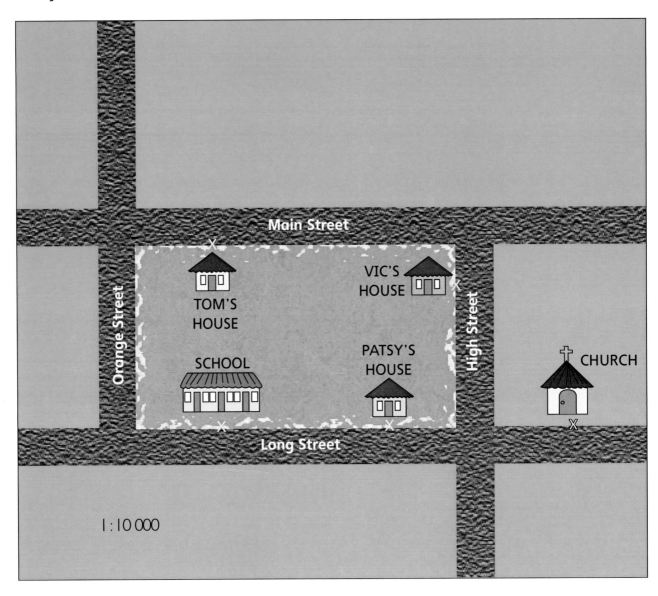

1 Work out the following distances in metres. Measure along the roads.

   a from Tom's house to school   **b** from Vic's house to school

   c from Patsy's house to school   **d** from Tom's house to Vic's house

   e from Vic's house to church   **f** from Patsy's house to church

   g from Patsy's house to Vic's house   **h** from Tom's house to church

2 **a** What is the shortest route from Tom's house to Patsy's house?

   b How far is this in metres?

Working with scale measurements

This map shows the roads in a small town.

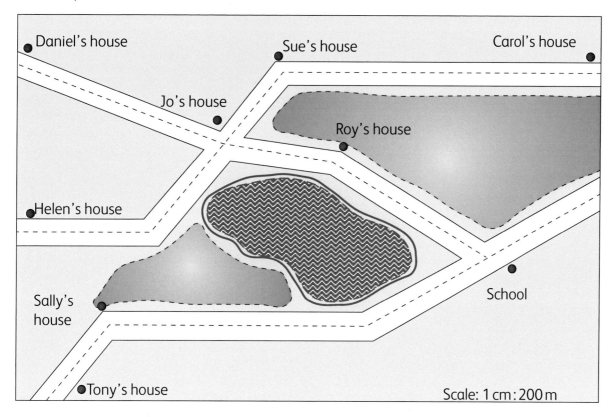

1 Work out the following distances in metres. Measure along the roads.

    a from Carol's house to Tony's house   **b** from Sally's house to school

    c from Sally's house to Carol's house   **d** from Daniel's house to Tony's house

    e from Roy's house to Tony's house   **f** from Jo's house to school

2 Sue and Carol walk across the field to get to school.

    a How many metres does Sue walk?   **b** How many metres does Carol walk?

    c If they walked along the road, how
        much longer would their routes be?

3 Answer these scale problems.

    a On a map, paper, 1 cm represents 5 km.
        If the actual distance between two towns is 40 km, what is the length on paper?

    b The actual distance between two islands is 96 km.
        If 1 cm on a map represents 6 km, what is the length on the map?

    c The actual distance between two towns is 55 km.
        If 1 cm on paper represents 10 km, what is the length on paper?

    d On a house plan, 1 cm represents 4 metres.
        If the length of the house is 30 metres, what is the length on the plan?

Scale drawings

Explain

When we draw maps and plans, we usually have to fit the drawing into a much smaller space on the paper than it takes up in real life.

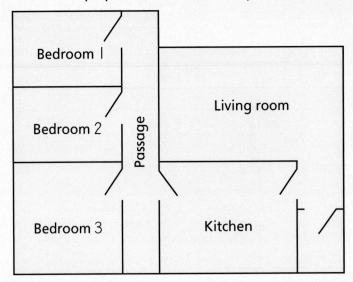

The **scale** of this sketch is 1 : 80.
That means 1 cm on the sketch represents 80 cm in real life.

1 Measure the following lengths on the plan. Multiply by 80 to work out the lengths in real life in centimetres.

   a the lengths of the bedrooms

   b the width of bedroom 1

   c the width of bedroom 2

   d the width of bedroom 3

   e the width of each door opening

   f the length and width of the living room

   g the length and width of the kitchen

   h the length and width of the passage

2 Convert all the lengths from Question 1 into metres.

3 If I want to cover the floor of each bedroom in wall-to-wall carpeting, how many square metres of carpet will I need?

4 If I want to tile the living room, how many square metres of tiles will I need?

Try this

Challenge yourself to draw your school or community to scale.

Time

The 24-hour clock

> ### Explain
>
> A day starts at midnight, which is 00:00. In the diagram, the **a.m.** hours are shown on the inner clock.
> The **p.m.** hours are shown on the outer clock.
> The 12 a.m. hours and 12 p.m. hours make 24 hours.
>
> 1:00 a.m. is 1 hour after midnight and is written as 01:00
> 2:30 a.m. is 2 hours and 30 minutes after midnight and is written as 02:30
> 12:30 a.m. is half an hour after midnight and is written as 00:30
> 1:00 p.m. is 13 hours after midnight and is written as 13:00
> 2:30 p.m. is 14 hours and 30 minutes after midnight and is written as 14:30
> 10:15 p.m. is 22 hours and 15 minutes after midnight and is written as 22:15

1 Copy and complete the table.

	Time	24-hour clock
a	4:00 a.m.	04:00
b	5:00 a.m.	
c		06:30
d		07:15
e	11:45 a.m.	
f	12:00 noon	

2 Write these 24-hour clock times using a.m.

   a 08:18   **b** 06:20   **c** 01:30
   d 03:10   **e** 09:05   **f** 00:05

3 Copy and complete the table.

	Time	24-hour clock
a	6:00 p.m.	18:00
b	7:00 p.m.	
c	10:00 p.m.	
d		21:30
e	11:45 p.m.	
f	12:00 midnight	

4 Write these 24-hour clock times using p.m.

   a 16:00   **b** 13:30   **c** 18:15
   d 21:17   **e** 19:08   **f** 14:15

5 Look at the airline timetable.
It shows the times that four planes leave Toronto and arrive in Antigua.

   a Which is the fastest flight?

   b Which is the slowest flight?

   c Make another timetable showing these times, using a.m. and p.m. What do you notice about the 24-hour clock and the a.m./p.m. clock?

Flight	Leaves Toronto	Arrives Antigua
CPM-1	10:05	16:30
CPM-2	14:15	21:50
CPM-3	15:30	23:20
CPM-4	16:45	22:40

Time problems

1 a Lillian left Kingston at 8:20 a.m. and arrived in Toronto at 3:40 p.m. At what times did she leave Kingston and arrive in Toronto, using the 24-hour clock?

  b How many hours and minutes did the journey take?

2 In 1944 Herb McKinley completed the Blue Mountain Marathon in 4:57:21.

Fifty years later Donald Quarry ran the same race in 3:32:09.

How much longer did it take to complete the race in 1944?

Cooking Times	
Pork	20 min. per lb
Chicken	19 min. per lb
Beef	28 min. per lb

3 The cooking times for some meats are given above.

  a A 6 lb chicken was placed on the grill at 3:25 p.m.
At what time should the chicken have finished cooking?

  b How long will it take to complete the cooking of 2.5 lb of beef?

  c What is the difference in time to cook 3.5 lb of pork and 4 lb of chicken?

4 An international cross-country relay race started at 13:30. This table shows the total time each team took to finish the race.

  a Use the table to work out the finishing time of each team.

  b Write them in order, starting with the winning team.

Team	Total time
Antigua	3 hours 27 minutes
Belize	2 hours 54 minutes
Barbados	3 hours 18 minutes
Costa Rica	3 hours 41 minutes
Jamaica	2 hours 57 minutes
Trinidad and Tobago	3 hours 4 minutes

Position	Team	Finishing time
1st		

5 Calculate the time difference between the teams that finished in these positions:

  a 1st → 6th   **b** 2nd → 3rd

  c 4th → 5th   **d** 1st → 2nd

6 Perimeter

Perimeters

Perimeter is the distance around a shape.
The perimeter is the sum of the
lengths of all the sides of a shape.
The perimeter of this shape is
12 cm + 3 cm + 12 cm + 3 cm = 30 cm

12 cm
3 cm   3 cm
12 cm

1 Measure these to work out the
perimeter of each shape in centimetres.

a

b

c

2 Measure the sides of these shapes in
millimetres and calculate each perimeter.

a

b

c

3 Harry ran around the perimeter of
this field.
How many metres did he run?

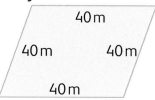

40 m
40 m   40 m
40 m

4 This church is built opposite an
L-shaped piece of land.
What is the perimeter of the land?

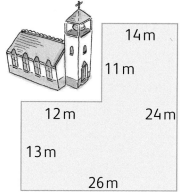

14 m
11 m
12 m   24 m
13 m
26 m

5 Andrew plans to go to Montego Bay
from St Ann's Bay and then return home.
He travels 12 km to Falmouth, then
15 km to Montego Bay. On his return
he travels 18 km to Savanna-la-Mar,
13 km to Black River, then
16 km back to St Ann's Bay.
How many km does he travel
altogether?

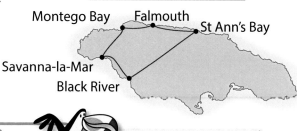

Montego Bay   Falmouth
St Ann's Bay
Savanna-la-Mar
Black River

Try this

Tell a classmate how you would go about
measuring the perimeter of a shape.

Finding perimeters

1 These shapes are not drawn to scale. Calculate the perimeter of each shape using the measurements given in the drawings.

a
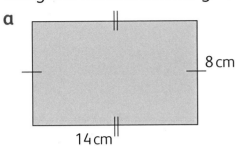
8 cm

14 cm

b
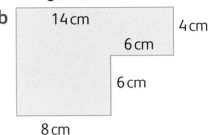
14 cm
4 cm
6 cm
6 cm
8 cm

c
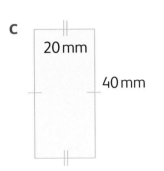
20 mm
40 mm

d
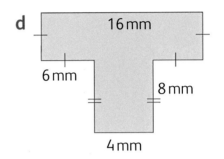
16 mm
6 mm
8 mm
4 mm

2 a Calculate the perimeter of this shape.

b One side of a square lawn measures 10 metres. What is the perimeter of the lawn?

c The width of a rectangular field is 8 metres. Its length is twice the width. What is the perimeter of the field?

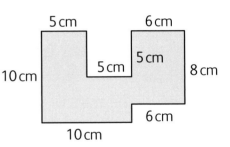
5 cm
6 cm
5 cm
5 cm
10 cm
8 cm
6 cm
10 cm

3 A rectangle measures 12 cm by 6 cm.

a What is the perimeter of the rectangle?

b If a square has the same perimeter as the rectangle, what is the length of one side?

4 The perimeter of a rectangle is 48 cm. If the width of the rectangle is 6 cm, what is the length?

5 The length of rectangle A is 7.4 cm and the width is 4.8 cm. The perimeter of rectangle B is 14.9 cm. How much longer is the perimeter of rectangle A than the perimeter of rectangle B?

Try this

There are shapes all around you: your classroom, your backyard, the church you attend. Why not measure each of them and find out which is the biggest and by how much?

Working with perimeters

1 Look at the bird's-eye view of a geometrically designed garden.

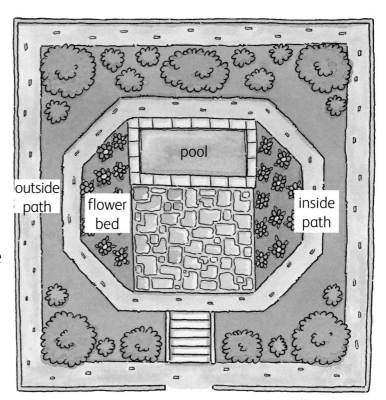

a The whole garden is a square, with each side 50 metres long.
What is the perimeter of the whole garden?

b Janet walks around the outside path three times.
How many metres does she walk?

c The length of Janet's step is 80 cm.
How many steps does she take to walk around the outside path once?

2 An album is 20 cm long and 14 cm wide.
Sal uses some lace to make an edge around the cover of the album.
She has 12 cm left over afterwards.
How long was her piece of lace?

3 The perimeter of a rectangular pool is 44 metres.
The length of the pool is 12 metres.

a What is the width of the pool?

b If Janet wants to put a fence around the two short sides and one long side of the pool, how many metres of fence does she need?

4 A rectangular table top has a length of 2.1 metres and a width of 1.3 metres.

a What is the perimeter of the table top?

b If Mark puts two of these tables next to each other, with the short sides touching, what is the combined perimeter of the table tops?

7 Geometry

Comparing and classifying shapes

Two-dimensional (2-D) shapes are flat.
They are also known as plane shapes.
They have only two dimensions – length and
width. The space taken up by a flat shape is
its **area**.

Three-dimensional (3-D) shapes have
length, width and height. They are also
known as solid shapes. The space taken
up by a solid shape is its **volume**.

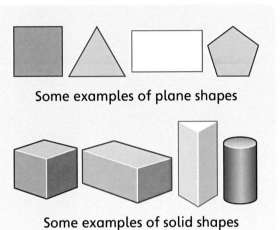

Some examples of plane shapes

Some examples of solid shapes

1 Copy and complete the table.
Tick in the correct column to classify each shape.

Shape		2-D	3-D
a	△		
b	◻		
c	╱		
d	⬠		
e	◁		
f	☕		

Shape		2-D	3-D
g	●		
h	◇		
i	▯		
j	▱		
k	▮		
l	T		

Try this game. Each player gets one minute to write down as many 2-D
and 3-D shapes as they can identify in the classroom. After the minute, the
student with the greatest total wins.

Classifying plane shapes and solids

Plane shapes may have three or more sides. The points where two straight sides meet are called corners or **vertices**. Angles are formed at the corners or vertices.

A **polygon** is a closed shape with sides made up of line segments. Polygons are classified according to the number of their sides.

A solid is an object that takes up space. The flat surfaces of a solid are called **faces**, and the line along which two faces meet is called an **edge**. Three or more edges may meet at the vertices. A **polyhedron** is a solid shape whose faces are all polygons. Some solid shapes have a flat face on which the shape rests. This is known as the **base**.

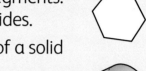

base   curved surface

This solid has 12 edges, 8 vertices and 6 faces

edge
edge
vertex

This solid has two circular faces which form bases. They are joined by a curved surface.

1 Copy and complete the table. Use the names in the box below to help.

Shape	Name	Is it 2-D or 3-D?
a		
b		
c		
d		
e		
f		

Shape	Name	Is it 2-D or 3-D?
g		
h		
i		
j		
k		

triangle	pentagon	cuboid	pyramid	hexagon
cylinder	sphere	cone	octagon	hexagonal prism	cube

Try this

Find out what the following shapes are. For an extra challenge, try to draw them!

a nonagon   **b** dodecagon   **c** undecagon

Solids

Explain

A **solid** is an object that takes up space. Solids have length, width and height. Talk about the similarities and differences of these shapes.

Cube		A cube is a prism with six square faces. Opposite faces are parallel. All faces meet at 90° angles.
Cone		A cone has a circular base and a curved surface that ends in one point called the apex.
Cylinder		A cylinder has two parallel circular faces that are the same size.
Prism		A prism is a polyhedron with two parallel polygon-shaped faces that are the same size. The other faces that join these parallel faces are rectangles. A prism is named by the shape of its end faces. This is a triangular prism.
Pyramid		A pyramid is a polyhedron with one base. The triangular faces that come from the base meet at an apex. A pyramid is named by the shape of its base. This is a square-based pyramid.

1 Mark and cut straight across an orange, as shown here.

 a What kind of solid is an orange?

 b What is the shape of the cut surface?

2 Name the shape of the surface that would be formed by cutting each of these solids straight across.

 a a cone   b a cube   c a cylinder (widthways)   d a cylinder (lengthways)

Try this

Use straws, card and sticky tape to make models of some solid shapes. Examine them carefully, then copy and complete a table like this.

Shape	Number of faces	Number of vertices	Number of edges
cube			
cuboid			

Nets of solids

Explain

The faces of a solid form its **net**. Imagine that you fold up a flat shape to form the 3-D shape. If you open it out, you will see a flat shape made up of the faces of the 3-D shape.

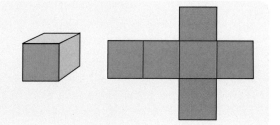

1 Copy the following nets onto squared paper or thin card.
Then cut out the nets along the solid lines, fold along the dotted lines and use tape to make the solid.
Name the solids you have made.

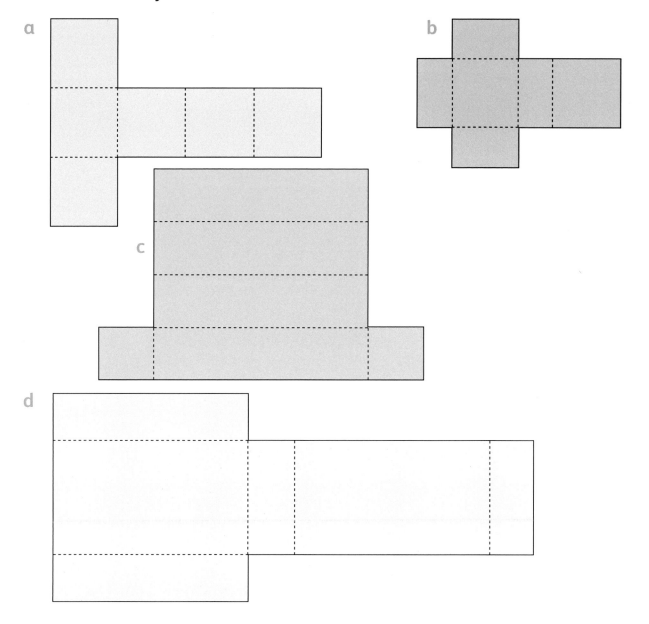

a

b

c

d

More nets of solids

1 Match the nets in column A to the solids in column B.

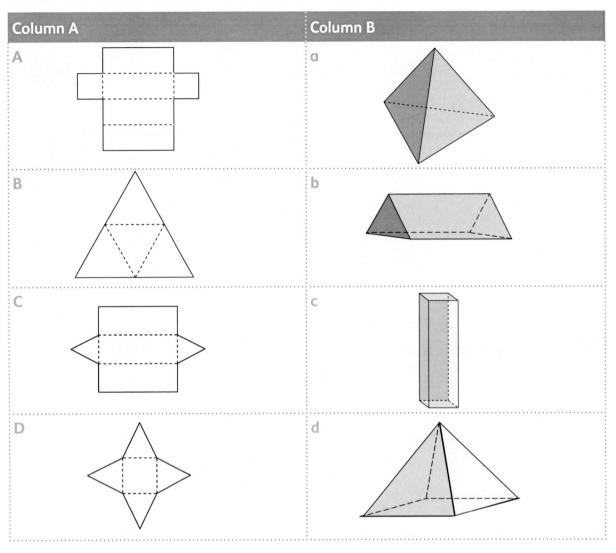

Column A	Column B
A	a
B	b
C	c
D	d

2 Use two of the nets shown above to construct a pyramid and a triangular prism. You can trace them or enlarge them.

3 Look at these shapes.
  What solids were combined to make them?

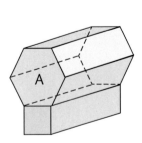
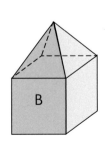
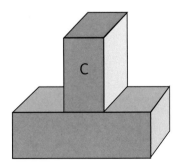

Cylinders and cones

1 Copy these nets onto paper or thin card.
  Use scissors and tape to help you make each solid.

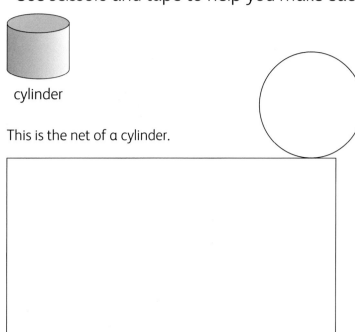

cylinder

This is the net of a cylinder.

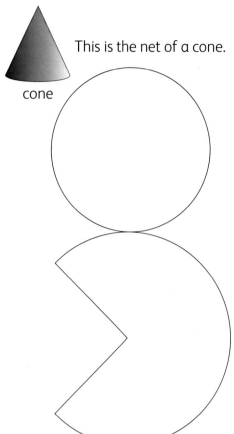

cone

This is the net of a cone.

Try this

Can you make a cone with an open base?
Draw a circle on a piece of paper or thin card.
Cut out half of the circle.
Now fold the remaining piece to make a cone.

Talk about

It is trickier to construct nets of cylinders and cones because of their circular faces. Discuss with your classmates the different ways you could construct these shapes. There is always more than one way to construct the net of a solid!

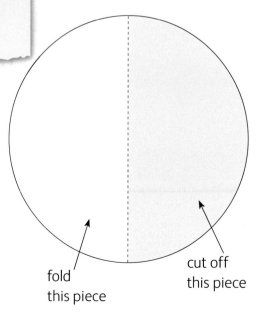

fold
this piece

cut off
this piece

35

Pyramids and prisms

1 Pyramids and prisms are special polyhedra.
What are the similarities and differences between the shapes?

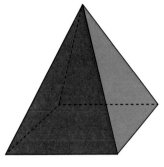

square-based pyramid

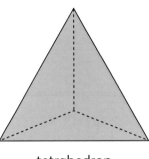

tetrahedron

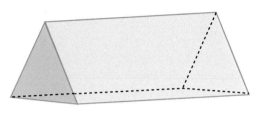

triangular prism

2 Copy the following nets onto paper or thin card.

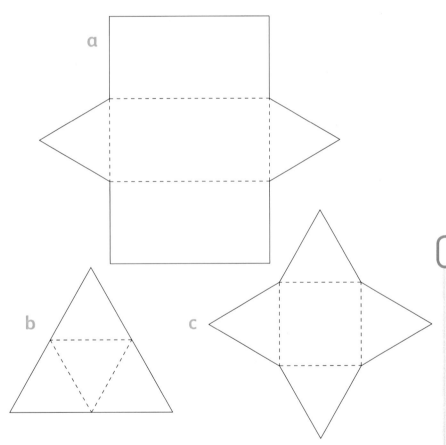

a

b

c

3 Now cut out the nets and make the solids.
Name the solids you have made.

> ## Remember
>
> Pyramids have a polygon base and triangular faces that meet at one of the vertices, called an apex. The base of the pyramid is used to name the pyramid, for example a square-based pyramid.
>
> Prisms have matching polygon ends, joined by rectangle faces. A prism has the same cross-section all the way along its length.

Solving problems using geometric models

1 Name the solids that can be constructed from these nets.

a 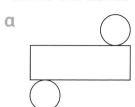   b 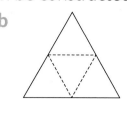   c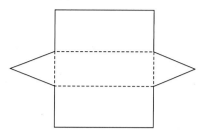

Imagine that you need to make some models using the following 3-D shapes.

A    B 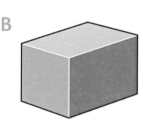   C 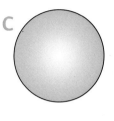   D 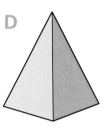   E

cylinder   cuboid   sphere   pyramid   triangular prism

2 Which solids would you use to construct a model of the human body?
Say which shapes you would use for:

   a the head   b the arms   c the body   d the legs.

3 Which solids would you use to construct a house?
Say which shapes you would use for:

   a the walls   b the roof.

4 Jane has made these models.   a   b   c

   a What 2-D shape has she used
     to build each model?

   b Try to work out how many
     faces each shape has.

 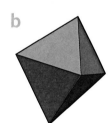 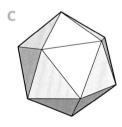

Reasoning activity

Which of these shapes would best fill the orange box, without leaving any
spaces? Discuss your answers with your class.

2 cm

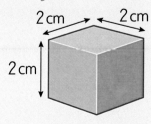
2 cm 2 cm
2 cm

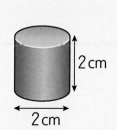
2 cm
2 cm

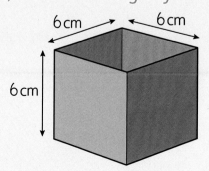
6 cm 6 cm
6 cm

Data

Data collection

Another name for information is **data**. We can obtain data from many sources – from listening to our friends, families and teachers, from our own observations, and from the media.

1 What is your favourite TV show?

2 a What do you think are the favourite TV shows of your classmates?

   b How would you find out this information?

3 a Find out the favourite TV show of each student in your class.

   b Make a list of all the shows they named and how many students named each show as their favourite. Write the information in a table like this.

TV show	Number of students

4 a What is the most popular show among your classmates?

   b What is the least popular show among your classmates?

   c What else can you deduce from the information you found?

Surveys

Look at the collection of items in the picture.

1 Explain which of these items would be useful for finding out:

   a How many roads are in the main city in your parish?

   b Would the inhabitants of your town like a new hotel to be built on the main road?

   c How many cars stop at a particular set of traffic lights within five minutes?

2 Explain how each of the items can help people to gather information.

Reasoning activity

Work in pairs. Go to a road near your school where you can safely observe passing traffic. For 15 minutes, observe the vehicles that pass by. Fill out a table like the one below.

Use tallies to record the colour of each vehicle that passes. After fifteen minutes, add up how many vehicles of each colour went past.

Colour of vehicle	Tally	Total
red	IIII IIII IIII	15

Talk about

How would you find out how many vehicles of each colour pass through your main town in an hour?

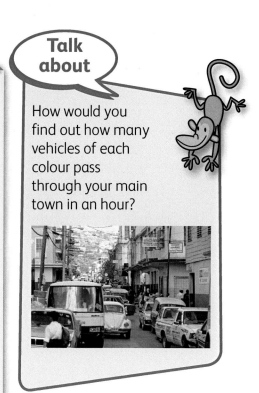

   a What was the most common colour?

   b What was the least common colour?

   c What was the difference in number between vehicles of the most common colour and the least common colour?

   d What conclusions can you draw from your vehicle survey?

Mean

Explain

The **mean** of a set of values = $\dfrac{\text{sum of the values}}{\text{number of values}}$

This table shows how ten students scored in their science test.

Name	Jenny	Linda	George	Leslie	Dick	Andy	Jill	Terence	Gina	Sally
Score out of 30	20	17	25	29	30	21	19	22	30	24

The sum of their scores = 20 + 17 + 25 + 29 + 30 + 21 + 19 + 22 + 30 + 24 = 237

The number of values is the number of scores: 10

$\dfrac{\text{sum of the values}}{\text{number of values}} = \dfrac{237}{10} = 237 \div 10 = 23.7$

The mean score is 23.7

1 The table shows how much money Jill saved each month for a year.

Jan	Feb	Mar	Apr	May	June
$8.00	$9.00	$7.00	$7.00	$5.00	$6.00

July	Aug	Sept	Oct	Nov	Dec
$10.00	$8.00	$9.00	$6.00	$7.00	$8.00

a What was Jill's mean saving for the first six months?

b What was Jill's mean saving for the last six months?

c You should be able to work out Jill's mean for the two-month period of March and April without any calculations.
What is the mean?

d Explain how you found the mean.

2 Work out the mean of each set of numbers.

a 3, 14, 26, 37, 43, 51   b 9, 6, 28, 32, 60   c 15, 90, 89, 67, 56

3 Work out the mean age of students in your class.

4 Measure the heights (in centimetres) of the students in your class.
Record the information in a table.

5 Use the information from Question 4 to answer these questions.

a What is the mean height of the boys?

b What is the mean height of the girls?

c What is the mean height of the whole class?

Talk about

What have you noticed about finding the mean?

Mode

Talk about

Which number occurs most often? Does it help to put the numbers in order?

Explain

The **mode** of a set of value is the value that occurs the most often.
For example: In the set   5, 8, 2, 3, 2, 2,   the mode is 2.
A set may have more than one mode.
For example: In the set   4, 5, 5, 6, 8, 8, 9,   the modes are 5 and 8.

1 In a gymnastics competition, these were the scores for each competitor.

Competitor A
7.1, 8.2, 8.4, 8.5, 7.1, 8.6

Competitor B
9.1, 9.9, 9.5, 8.5, 9.8, 8.5

Competitor C
6.5, 5.9, 7.2, 7.2, 5.9, 6.5

Competitor D
7.6, 7.7, 7.8, 8.2, 8.2, 7.5

  a Find the mode for each competitor's scores.

  b Find the overall mode.

  c Find the mean of each competitor's scores.'

2 For each of the following sets, find the mode.

  a 89, 95, 99, 99, 190, 199, 200   b 165, 120, 121, 159, 120, 121

  c 6, 6, 6, 7, 7, 8, 8, 9, 9, 9, 10, 11, 11, 11, 11   d 45, 56, 65, 65, 76, 78

  e 1.1, 1.2, 1.1, 1.1, 1.3, 1.3, 1.5, 1.3, 1.2, 1.6, 1.2, 1.5, 1.2

Reasoning activity

Do you think the competitors should receive their official score from the mean or from the mode of their six scores? Explain your answer to justify your reasoning.

More about the mode

A group of students were practising getting the basketball into the basket. Each student had ten tries. This is how many baskets they each made.

Name	Number of baskets
Jenny	卌
David	卌 ‖
Michelle	‖
Dinah	‖‖
Gareth	
Sue	卌 ‖‖
Benjamin	卌 卌
Harry	‖‖‖
Joe	‖‖
Mike	卌 ‖

Name	Number of baskets
Lisa	卌 ‖
Billy	卌 ‖
Tina	卌 ‖‖
Amal	卌 卌
Linda	‖‖‖
Dan	卌 ‖‖‖
Gary	卌 ‖‖‖
Wayne	卌 ‖‖
Andrew	卌 ‖
Liz	卌 ‖‖

1 What was the mode of their scores?

Reasoning activity

a Go outside and practise getting a ball through a basket or hoop. Another way to play this game is to practise throwing a coin into an empty tin. Each student should get ten chances.

b Make tally charts to record each student's score.

c Find the mode of the scores.

d Draw a bar chart to show the scores.

e What conclusions can you draw from your results?

2 Carry out a survey of the students in your class.

  a Find out the age of everyone in your class.
    Work out the mode of the ages.

  b Find out how many brothers and sisters your classmates have.
    Work out the mode.

  c Ask 30 different people what month they were born in.
    Draw a bar graph showing your findings.
    Work out the mode.

Talk about

What have you noticed about the mode?

Median

Let's do the number in the middle!

median

Explain

If we arrange a set of values in order of size, starting with the smallest, the **median** is the middle value.

In groups of five, stand in order of height. Who is the median?

If a set has an even number of values, the median is the value halfway between the two middle values when the set is ordered.

1 Identify the middle number in each of the sets below.

   a 1, 2, 3, 4, 5   **b** 2, 4, 6, 8, 10, 12, 14

   c 3, 6, 9, 12, 15, 18, 21, 24, 27   **d** 4, 5, 9, 11, 13

2 Find the median of each set.

   a (12) (13) (19)   **b** (28) (30) (31) (33) (40) (42) (50)

   c (99) (101) (160) (161) (180)   **d** (122) (125) (128) (131) (134) (137)

3 First arrange each set of numbers in order of size. Then find the median.

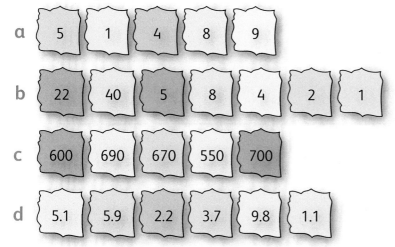

   a 5   1   4   8   9

   b 22   40   5   8   4   2   1

   c 600   690   670   550   700

   d 5.1   5.9   2.2   3.7   9.8   1.1

Stem-and-leaf plots

Stem-and-leaf plots are formed by splitting numbers collected into two parts, tens and ones. The tens digits form the stem and the ones digits form the leaves.

For example:

The table on the left shows the scores of eight students in an English test. The diagram on the right shows the data in a stem-and-leaf plot.

Name	Score
Mark	43
Jill	64
Lillian	73
Raymond	54
Paul	67
Rhona	78
Lorna	49
Samuel	77

Stem	Leaf
2	
3	
4	3 9
5	4
6	4 7
7	3 7 8
8	

Stem-and-leaf plots are used to compare the frequencies of different values in a set of data.

Some Grade 6 students bought bottles of water in different stores. These are the prices (in dollars) of the bottles they bought.

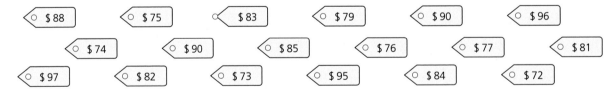

$88 $75 $83 $79 $90 $96
$74 $90 $85 $76 $77 $81
$97 $82 $73 $95 $84 $72

1 Represent the data in a stem-and-leaf plot.

Stem	Leaf

2 Find the mode, median and mean values.

3 Which leaf in the stem-and-leaf plot corresponds to the minimum price? Which one corresponds to the maximum price?

More about stem-and-leaf plots

1 Use these scores from two science tests to answer the questions.

Science Test 1

Stem	Leaf
6	2 3 4 5 5 6
7	0 1 3 9 9 9
8	2 3 7 8
9	1 3 5

Science Test 2

Stem	Leaf
5	6 9
6	0 4 5
7	0 0 7 8 9
8	3 5 5 7
9	2 6

a The passing score is 70. How many students passed each test?

b How many did not pass each test?

c Which of the two tests had the higher median score?

2 This table shows the numbers of runs made by 9 cricketers.

Player	1	2	3	4	5	6	7	8	9
Number of runs	34	22	9	3	12	19	31	12	11

a Represent the data in a stem-and-leaf plot.

Stem	Leaf

b What are the mode, median and mean values?

3 Here are the times (in seconds) taken by some students to run 100 m.

15.1	15.2	15.2	14.3	12.8	15.1	14.4	16.5
16.0	16.6	15.9	15.8	12.5	12.4	18.1	13.8
16.6	15.7	14.2	13.9	13.2	13.4	13.5	14.0

Draw a stem-and-leaf plot for this data.

Talk about

Discuss in pairs and write four ways you may use a stem-and-leaf plot in real life.

45

9 Primes, composites, factors and multiples

Odd, even, prime and composite numbers

Talk about

What do you know about these types of numbers?

| odd numbers | even numbers | composite numbers | whole numbers | prime numbers | factors |

1 Copy and complete this table by putting a ✔ in the correct columns.

Number	Odd	Even	Prime	Composite
24		✔		✔
38				
83				
15				
21				

Number	Odd	Even	Prime	Composite
46				
17				
64				
91				
82				

2 Find the products. Then use your answers to copy and complete the rule.

a 4 × 6 =   **b** 2 × 10 =   **c** 4 × 8 =   **d** 6 × 8 =   **e** 10 × 6 =

Rule: Even number × even number = _____ number

3 Find the products. Then use your answers to copy and complete the rule.

a 7 × 3 =   **b** 1 × 5 =   **c** 9 × 5 =   **d** 3 × 11 =   **e** 13 × 7 =

Rule: Odd number × odd number = _____ number

4 Make up five multiplications of your own for this rule. Then copy and complete it.

Rule: Odd number × even number = _____ number

5 List each set of numbers.

a {odd numbers less than 20}   **b** {even numbers less than 20}

c {prime numbers less than 20}   **d** {composite numbers less than 20}

Reasoning activity

a Only one even number is prime. Which number is it?

b Is 1 a prime number? Give reasons for your answer.

c Does the sum of three consecutive odd numbers give you an odd or an even answer? Explain why.

d Does the sum of three consecutive even numbers give you an odd or an even answer? Explain why.

Factors, prime factors and the HCF

Explain

A **factor** of a given number is a number that divides into the given number and leaves no remainder.

For example: The factors of 6 are 1, 2, 3 and 6.

A **prime number** is a number whose only factors are 1 and itself.

A **prime factor** is a factor that is a prime number.

For example: 7 is a prime number. The prime factors of 6 are 2 and 3.

The **highest common factor** (**HCF**) of a set of numbers is the highest number that divides into each of the numbers in the set without leaving a remainder.

1 Write all the factors of each number.

   a 42   **b** 38   **c** 30   **d** 90   **e** 100

2 Write all the factors of 12 and of 45. Circle the prime factors.

3 Copy and complete this table.

	Number	Factors	Prime factors
a	16	1, 2, 4, 8, 16	2
b	20		
c	30		

	Number	Factors	Prime factors
d	18		
e	65		
f	42		

4 The HCF of 6 and 15 is 3. The HCF of 14 and 21 is 7. Can you explain why?

5 Find the HCF of each set of numbers.

   a 20 and 24   **b** 36 and 27   **c** 12, 18 and 30

6 a What is the largest number that divides into 42 and 48 without leaving a remainder?

   b What is the largest number that divides into 26 and 37 leaving a remainder of 4 in each case?

Explain

These are **factor trees**. The main branches show the factors of the number in the trunk. The smaller branches show the factors of the numbers in the main branches. We can express a number as the product of its prime factors. This is called **prime factorisation**.

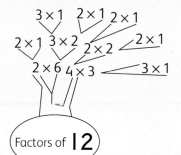

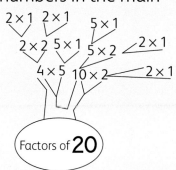

7 Draw a factor tree for each number and express it as a product of its prime factors.

   a 24   **b** 18   **c** 28   **d** 36   **e** 50   **f** 120   **g** 225   **h** 196

Expressing numbers using prime factors

Explain

You learned about using powers on page 13. Powers are also called **exponents**.
We can use exponents to express composite numbers as the products of their primes.

For example: Express 12 as the product of primes in exponential form.

Method 1

Divide 12 by its prime factors in a grid:

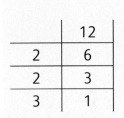

Put 12 in the right-hand column.
The lowest prime that goes into 12 is 2.
$12 \div 2 = 6$. Write the 6 under the 12.
The lowest prime that goes into 6 is 2.
$6 \div 2 = 3$. Write the 3 under the 6.
The lowest prime that goes into 3 is 3.
$3 \div 3 = 1$.
So $12 = 2 \times 2 \times 3$

We can also express 2×2 in exponential form as 2^2. So $12 = 2^2 \times 3$

Method 2

Use a factor tree:

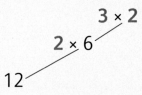

The prime factors of 12 are 2, 3 and 2, or $12 = 2 \times 2 \times 3$
In exponential form, $12 = 2^2 \times 3$

1 Write each of these numbers as a product of primes in exponential form.

a 6	**b** 14	**c** 24	**d** 36	**e** 40	**f** 120
g 236	**h** 498	**i** 56	**j** 1 624	**k** 2 000	**l** 500

2 Work in pairs. Each partner must write their list of composite numbers as the product of primes in exponential form. Check each other's answers.

Partner 1:   **a** 4   **b** 49   **c** 225   **d** 400   **e** 36   **f** 48

Partner 2:   **a** 9   **b** 81   **c** 180   **d** 16   **e** 324   **f** 25

Multiples and the LCM

Explain

The **multiples** of a number *x* are numbers which are exactly divisible by *x*.
For example:
The multiples of 2 are 2, 4, 6, 8, 10, 12, 14, 16, 18, 20, …
The **common multiple** of a set of numbers is a multiple shared by all of the numbers.
For example:
10 and 20 are common multiples of 2 and 5.
12 is a common multiple of 2, 3, 4 and 6.
The **lowest common multiple** (**LCM**) of a set of numbers is the smallest number that is exactly divisible by each number in the set.
For example:
The multiples of 2 are 2, 4, 6, 8, 10, …
The multiples of 3 are 3, 6, 9, 12, 15, …
The LCM of 2 and 3 is 6. This is the lowest multiple common to both numbers.

1 The multiples of 8 are 8, 16, 24, 32, 40, 48, …

The multiples of 12 are 12, 24, 36, 48, …

The LCM of 8 and 12 is 24. Why?

2 In the same way, find the LCM of each of these sets of numbers.

   a 5 and 6   **b** 2, 3 and 4

3 a Copy the diagram.

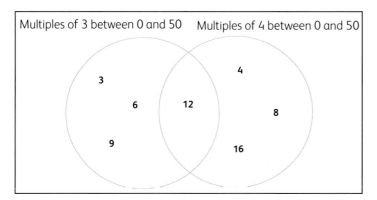

Fill in the missing multiples in each of the circled sets.

Fill in the common multiples in the overlapping area between the sets.

  b Underline the lowest common multiple.

Finding the LCM using prime factorisation

Explain

Find the LCM of 12 and 18 using prime factorisation.
First write each number as a product of its prime factors.
12 = 2 × 2 × 3   18 = 2 × 3 × 3
You then need to multiply these prime factors together. If they appear more than once, you just include the highest number of times it occurs.
12: 2 occurs twice.   18: 3 occurs twice.
Multiply them: 2 × 2 × 3 × 3
So the LCM of 12 and 18 is 2 × 2 × 3 × 3 = 36

1 Find the LCM of each set of numbers using prime factorisation.

   a 25 and 30   **b** 12 and 14   **c** 4, 6 and 8
   d 5, 7 and 8   **e** 7, 9 and 12   **f** 15, 20 and 24

Reasoning activity

A scientist has built a machine with screens, lights, bells and flags.

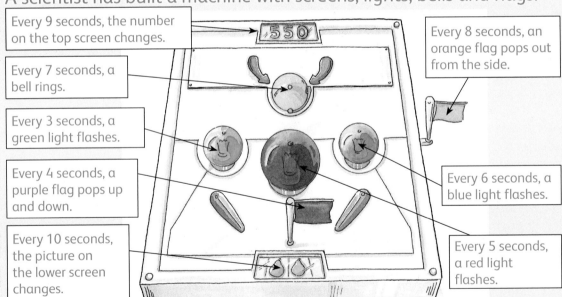

Every 9 seconds, the number on the top screen changes.

Every 7 seconds, a bell rings.

Every 3 seconds, a green light flashes.

Every 4 seconds, a purple flag pops up and down.

Every 10 seconds, the picture on the lower screen changes.

Every 8 seconds, an orange flag pops out from the side.

Every 6 seconds, a blue light flashes.

Every 5 seconds, a red light flashes.

Use prime factorisation to work out how many seconds it will be until:
a all three lights flash at the same time
b the number screen and the picture screen change at the same time
c both the flags pop out at the same time
d the green light flashes at the same time as the bell rings
e the number screen changes at the same time as the orange flag pops out.
   Make up two more questions about the machine's timing, and get your friend to answer them.

10 Fractions and decimals

Fractions

Explain

A fraction has three parts:
numerator, vinculum and denominator.

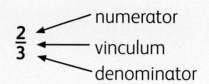

$\frac{2}{3}$ ← numerator
← vinculum
← denominator

1 Complete this chart to show proper fractions, improper fractions and mixed numbers.

(circle diagram)	$\frac{2}{3}$	proper fraction
	$\frac{13}{8}$	
	$3\frac{7}{9}$	
(three squares)		mixed number
(pinwheel square)	$\frac{7}{9}$	
	$\frac{9}{10}$	proper fraction

2 Write these improper fractions as mixed numbers.

   a $\frac{11}{3}$ **b** $\frac{19}{3}$ **c** $\frac{145}{12}$ **d** $\frac{169}{120}$ **e** $\frac{774}{50}$ **f** $\frac{45}{2}$

3 Write these mixed numbers as improper fractions.

   a $3\frac{3}{4}$ **b** $5\frac{1}{2}$ **c** $8\frac{1}{4}$ **d** $7\frac{2}{5}$ **e** $10\frac{1}{7}$ **f** $105\frac{2}{7}$

Explain

$3 \div 1 = 3$. So another way of writing 3 is $\frac{3}{1}$.

To find a **reciprocal**, interchange the denominator with the numerator.

So the reciprocal of 3 (or $\frac{3}{1}$) is $\frac{1}{3}$. The reciprocal of 18 is $\frac{1}{18}$.

The product of any number and its reciprocal is always 1 (one).

4 Write down the reciprocal of each number.

   a 6   **b** 10   **c** 24   **d** 17   **e** 9

5 Use the numbers 1, 2, 3, 7, 9 and 12 to write as many of these as you can:

   a proper fractions   **b** improper fractions   **c** mixed numbers.

   d Write the mixed numbers from part **c** as improper fractions.

   e Write the improper fractions from part **b** as mixed numbers.

LCD

Explain

The **lowest common denominator (LCD)** of a set of fractions is the lowest common multiple (LCM) of their denominators. For example:

Find the LCD of $\frac{1}{2}, \frac{1}{4}, \frac{5}{6}$.

The denominators are 2, 4 and 6. The LCM of 2, 4 and 6 is 12, so the LCD is 12.

We can rewrite the fractions using the LCD. This helps us to compare the fractions.

$$\frac{1}{2} = \frac{6}{12} \qquad\qquad \frac{1}{4} = \frac{3}{12} \qquad\qquad \frac{5}{6} = \frac{10}{12}$$

$\frac{3}{12} < \frac{6}{12} < \frac{10}{12}$ so $\frac{1}{4} < \frac{1}{2} < \frac{5}{6}$

1 Copy and complete this table. The first example has been done for you.

	Fractions	LCM of denominators	LCD of fractions	Fractions over LCD
a	$\frac{1}{5}, \frac{1}{4}$	20	20	$\frac{4}{20}, \frac{5}{20}$
b	$\frac{2}{5}, \frac{3}{10}, \frac{1}{15}$			
c	$\frac{1}{4}, \frac{1}{10}, \frac{2}{3}$			
d	$\frac{3}{2}, \frac{3}{4}, \frac{3}{8}$			
e	$\frac{3}{7}, \frac{2}{3}, \frac{5}{4}$			

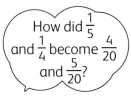

How did $\frac{1}{5}$ and $\frac{1}{4}$ become $\frac{4}{20}$ and $\frac{5}{20}$?

2 Write both fractions in each pair using the LCD.
Then write <, > or = between the fractions.

a $\frac{1}{2} \bigcirc \frac{8}{12}$ **b** $\frac{1}{2} \bigcirc \frac{5}{8}$ **c** $\frac{1}{4} \bigcirc \frac{2}{10}$ **d** $\frac{3}{12} \bigcirc \frac{1}{4}$ **e** $\frac{3}{6} \bigcirc \frac{1}{4}$ **f** $\frac{3}{5} \bigcirc \frac{2}{3}$

3 Write each of the following sets of fractions using the LCD of the set.

a $\frac{10}{11}, \frac{4}{5}$ **b** $\frac{1}{6}, \frac{3}{8}$ **c** $\frac{2}{9}, \frac{1}{3}, \frac{5}{6}$ **d** $\frac{17}{42}, \frac{13}{14}, \frac{3}{4}$

4 $\frac{1}{2}$ and $\frac{4}{8}$ are equivalent fractions.
Use the LCD to help you work out which fractions in each set are equivalent.

a $\frac{1}{2}, \frac{1}{4}, \frac{2}{4}, \frac{6}{12}, \frac{6}{10}$ **b** $\frac{1}{5}, \frac{3}{5}, \frac{5}{6}, \frac{6}{10}, \frac{30}{50}$ **c** $\frac{18}{20}, \frac{4}{9}, \frac{9}{10}, \frac{45}{50}, \frac{9}{20}$

d $\frac{12}{18}, \frac{1}{3}, \frac{3}{8}, \frac{5}{16}, \frac{9}{24}$ **e** $\frac{4}{8}, \frac{2}{7}, \frac{3}{4}, \frac{18}{36}, \frac{4}{14}$ **f** $\frac{1}{8}, \frac{6}{42}, \frac{4}{32}, \frac{3}{7}, \frac{12}{48}$

5 Copy and complete these equivalent fractions.

a $\frac{4}{9} = \frac{32}{\square}$ **b** $\frac{7}{12} = \frac{\square}{144}$ **c** $\frac{9}{13} = \frac{63}{\square}$ **d** $\frac{3}{\square} = \frac{12}{20}$

e $\frac{8}{\square} = \frac{2}{5}$ **f** $\frac{9}{27} = \frac{1}{\square}$ **g** $\frac{\square}{50} = \frac{4}{100}$ **h** $\frac{36}{48} = \frac{3}{\square}$

i $\frac{12}{15} = \frac{48}{\square}$ **j** $\frac{7}{\square} = \frac{49}{63}$ **k** $\frac{\square}{20} = \frac{48}{80}$ **l** $\frac{5}{9} = \frac{\square}{99}$

Reasoning activity

Which fraction is halfway between $\frac{1}{2}$ and $\frac{5}{6}$? How could you prove you are correct?

Adding fractions and mixed numbers

Explain

It is easy to add fractions or mixed numbers with the same denominator.

For example: $\frac{3}{7} + \frac{1}{7} = \frac{4}{7}$ Or: $2\frac{1}{5} + 6\frac{3}{5} = 8\frac{4}{5}$

When you want to add two fractions with different denominators, you need to find the LCD.

For example:
$$\frac{4}{5} + \frac{1}{2} + \frac{2}{3}$$
$$= \frac{24}{30} + \frac{15}{30} + \frac{20}{30}$$
$$= \frac{59}{30}$$
$$= 1\frac{29}{30}$$

$$2\frac{1}{4} + 1\frac{5}{6}$$
$$= 2 + 1 + \frac{1}{4} + \frac{5}{6}$$
$$= 3 + \frac{3}{12} + \frac{10}{12}$$
$$= 3 + \frac{13}{12}$$
$$= 3 + 1\frac{1}{12}$$
$$= 4\frac{1}{12}$$

When you are working with mixed numbers, add together the whole numbers first, then the fractions, and then combine the two.

1 Add these fractions and mixed numbers.

a $\frac{8}{9} + \frac{7}{9} + \frac{2}{9}$ **b** $\frac{5}{8} + \frac{1}{3}$ **c** $3\frac{4}{5} + 1\frac{1}{6}$ **d** $\frac{3}{4} + 2\frac{3}{7} + 1\frac{1}{2}$ **e** $3\frac{1}{7} + 4\frac{2}{3} + \frac{1}{5}$ **f** $\frac{22}{7} + \frac{5}{4} + \frac{15}{2}$

2 Find the sum.

a $4\frac{3}{10}$ and $1\frac{15}{12}$ **b** $7\frac{1}{2}$ and $3\frac{4}{5}$ **c** $1\frac{1}{3}$ and $\frac{2}{15}$

d $3\frac{1}{6}$ and $7\frac{3}{7}$ **e** $4\frac{5}{8}$ and $\frac{3}{4}$ **f** $2\frac{2}{5}$ and $3\frac{2}{3}$

3 Mrs James baked a round cake.
She gave $\frac{1}{3}$ of the cake to Sheila, $\frac{2}{5}$ to Agatha, and $\frac{1}{4}$ to George.

a Who received the largest piece?

b Who received the smallest piece?

c What fraction of the cake was left?

4 $\frac{7}{15}$ of the passengers on a plane went to Jamaica.

$\frac{1}{6}$ of the passengers went to Trinidad and $\frac{1}{5}$ of the passengers went to Barbados.

a What fraction of the passengers went to one of these destinations?

b What fraction of the passengers went to other destinations?

c What is the smallest number of seats the plane could have had? (Hint: use the LCD.)

Subtracting fractions and mixed numbers

Explain

As with addition, it is easy to subtract fractions with the same denominator.

For example: $\frac{3}{7} - \frac{1}{7} = \frac{2}{7}$ Or: $4\frac{8}{9} - 1\frac{1}{9} = 3\frac{7}{9}$

Finding the LCD helps us to find the difference between fractions that have different denominators.

For example:

$$\frac{4}{5} - \frac{2}{3}$$
$$= \frac{12}{15} - \frac{10}{15}$$
$$= \frac{2}{15}$$

$$2\frac{1}{4} - 1\frac{5}{6}$$
$$= \frac{9}{4} - \frac{11}{6}$$
$$= \frac{27}{12} - \frac{22}{12}$$
$$= \frac{5}{12}$$

$$2 - \frac{3}{8}$$
$$= \frac{16}{8} - \frac{3}{8}$$
$$= \frac{13}{8}$$
$$= 1\frac{5}{8}$$

1 Work out these.

a $\frac{11}{16} - \frac{5}{16}$ **b** $\frac{5}{9} - \frac{1}{4}$ **c** $4\frac{6}{7} - 2\frac{1}{3}$ **d** $3\frac{1}{2} - 2\frac{4}{15}$

e $10 - \frac{9}{10}$ **f** $3 - \frac{1}{3}$ **g** $\frac{24}{7} - \frac{61}{14}$ **h** $21 - \frac{7}{20}$

2 Work out these. Give your answers in their simplest form.

a $(\frac{5}{8} - \frac{1}{4}) + \frac{1}{2}$ **b** $(3\frac{5}{6} - 1\frac{1}{3}) + \frac{1}{2}$ **c** $(7\frac{7}{10} + \frac{3}{5}) - \frac{1}{2}$

d $(10\frac{7}{8} - 2\frac{1}{3}) + \frac{1}{9}$ **e** $(1\frac{19}{20} - \frac{1}{5}) + 5\frac{1}{2}$

3 a Emily gave her grandmother $\frac{2}{5}$ of a loaf of bread. What fraction of the bread was left?

b If Emily's loaf had 20 slices, how many slices did she give to her grandmother?

4 John gave $\frac{3}{8}$ of a box of plums to his mother, and $\frac{1}{5}$ his friend. $\frac{3}{10}$ of the box were bad, so he threw them away and ate the rest.

a What fraction of the plums did John give away?

b What fraction did John eat?

> **Talk about**
>
> What are the things to consider when subtracting fractions? Discuss why this rule is important:
>
> When adding or subtracting fractions with unlike denominators, first find the LCD.

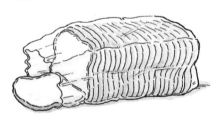

Multiplying fractions

Explain

There are different methods of multiplying fractions. For example:

$\frac{3}{4} \times \frac{1}{2}$

$= \frac{(3 \times 1)}{(4 \times 2)}$

$= \frac{3}{8}$

$\frac{5}{6}$ of 12

$= \frac{5}{6_1} \times \frac{12^2}{1}$

$= \frac{5 \times 2}{1 \times 1}$

$= 10$

$\frac{5^1}{8_4} \times \frac{6^1}{7} \times \frac{7^1}{15_1}$

$= \frac{1 \times 1 \times 1}{4 \times 7 \times 1}$

$= \frac{1}{28}$

$1\frac{3}{4} \times 2\frac{4}{7}$

$= \frac{7^1}{4_2} \times \frac{18^9}{7_1}$

$= \frac{9}{2}$

$= 4\frac{1}{2}$

Work out these. Give your answers as proper fractions or mixed numbers.

1 a $\frac{3}{10}$ of 250   **b** $5\frac{2}{3} \times \frac{3}{4}$ **c** $2\frac{1}{3} \times 4\frac{1}{5}$

   d $\frac{1}{3} \times 2\frac{1}{4} \times \frac{8}{9}$ **e** $3\frac{2}{5} \times 4\frac{1}{4} \times \frac{1}{8}$ **f** $7 \times \frac{8}{9}$

   g $\frac{1}{2} \times \frac{3}{5} - \frac{1}{4}$ **h** $\frac{11}{12} \times 1\frac{1}{7} + \frac{1}{3}$ **i** $(\frac{9}{8} - \frac{5}{6}) \times 1\frac{1}{2}$

2 Jenny had 24 grapes. She ate $\frac{1}{6}$ of them and gave $\frac{3}{4}$ of the rest to Tom.
   a How many grapes did Jenny eat?
   b How many grapes did she give to Tom?
   c How many grapes did she have left?

3 There are 320 T-shirts in a delivery box.
   $\frac{1}{5}$ of the T-shirts are red, $\frac{1}{4}$ of the T-shirts
   are green and $\frac{3}{8}$ of the T-shirts are blue.
   The rest of the T-shirts are white.
   a How many T-shirts are red?
   b How many T-shirts are green?
   c How many T-shirts are blue?
   d What fraction of the T-shirts are white?

4 Work out these.
   a $\frac{4}{5} \times \frac{2}{2}$ **b** $\frac{6}{7} \times \frac{5}{5}$ **c** $\frac{7}{11} \times \frac{3}{3}$

5 Generate five equivalent fractions for each of
   these fractions.
   a $\frac{10}{11}$ **b** $\frac{77}{100}$ **c** $\frac{12}{15}$ **d** $\frac{19}{25}$

6 Find the value of n in each of these.
   a $\frac{1}{2} \times \frac{1}{3} = n$ **b** $4 \times \frac{2}{3} = n$ **c** $2\frac{1}{2} \times 2\frac{1}{2} = n$

Talk about

Look at your answers
to Question 4. In pairs,
write a rule about
creating equivalent
fractions.

Division of fractions

Explain

Division is the inverse operation of multiplication. To divide by a fraction, you multiply by the multiplicative inverse of the fraction. In other words, dividing by a fraction is the same as multiplying by the fraction 'upside down' or inverted.

The whole cake has 10 slices.

$1 \div \frac{1}{10}$

$= 1 \times \frac{10}{1}$

$= \frac{10}{1}$

$= 10$

$\frac{1}{2}$ of the cake has 5 slices.

$\frac{1}{2} \div \frac{1}{10}$

$= \frac{1}{2} \times \frac{10}{1}$

$= \frac{10}{2}$

$= 5$

$\frac{2}{5}$ of the cake has 4 slices.

$\frac{2}{5} \div \frac{1}{10}$

$= \frac{2}{5} \times \frac{10}{1}$

$= \frac{20}{5}$

$= 4$

1 Divide these.

a $2 \div \frac{1}{4}$ **b** $12 \div \frac{4}{5}$ **c** $6 \div \frac{2}{3}$ **d** $\frac{1}{4} \div 12$

e $\frac{1}{5} \div 15$ **f** $\frac{2}{3} \div 4$ **g** $2\frac{1}{2} \div \frac{1}{4}$ **h** $10\frac{1}{4} \div \frac{1}{2}$

Talk about

In America, a 25c coin is also called a 'quarter'. Why is this?

How many quarters are there in a dollar? In $10? In $100?

2 Answer these problems.

a $3\frac{1}{2}$ pies are shared equally among 6 children. What fraction of a pie does each child get?

b $\frac{3}{4}$ of a loaf must be shared among 5 people. What fraction of the loaf will each person be given?

c Shireen has $\frac{3}{4}$ kg of sweets. She puts them into smaller packets, each holding $\frac{1}{8}$ kg. How many packets does she fill?

d Annie has $\frac{3}{4}$ litre of juice. How many glasses can she fill if each glass holds $\frac{3}{10}$ of a litre?

Reciprocals

The **reciprocal** of a number is that number which, when multiplied by the number, gives 1. For example: $\frac{2}{3} \times \frac{3}{2} = \frac{6}{6} = 1$

To find the reciprocal of a number, you switch the denominator and numerator. Look at these examples:

The reciprocal of $\frac{2}{3}$ is $\frac{3}{2}$.
We flip (or invert) the fraction, like this:

$\frac{2}{3} \! \! \not\! \! \times \frac{3}{2}$

The reciprocal of 3 is $\frac{1}{3}$.
First convert the whole number to an improper fraction.

$3 = \frac{3}{1}$

$\frac{3}{1} \! \! \not\! \! \times \frac{1}{3}$

1 Write the reciprocals of these fractions.

  a $\frac{1}{2}$ **b** $\frac{1}{6}$ **c** $\frac{2}{7}$ **d** $\frac{5}{8}$ **e** $\frac{11}{12}$

  f $\frac{17}{24}$ **g** $\frac{36}{37}$ **h** $\frac{1}{100}$ **i** $\frac{127}{2}$ **j** $\frac{5}{9}$

2 Write the reciprocals of these whole numbers.

  a 5   **b** 10   **c** 3   **d** 7   **e** 45

3 Write these mixed numbers as improper fractions, then find their reciprocals.

  a $1\frac{1}{2}$ **b** $4\frac{4}{5}$ **c** $9\frac{9}{10}$ **d** $11\frac{2}{3}$ **e** $6\frac{7}{9}$

Now look what happens when we multiply a number by its reciprocal:

$\frac{1}{4} \times \frac{4}{1} = 1$

$\frac{3}{5} \times \frac{5}{3} = 1$

Dividing by a fraction is the same as multiplying by the reciprocal of the fraction:

$\frac{1}{2} \div \frac{4}{5}$

$= \frac{1}{2} \times \frac{5}{4}$

$= \frac{5}{8}$

Remember, you only use the reciprocal of the fraction after the ÷ sign.

4 Multiply these.

  a $\frac{2}{3} \times \frac{3}{2}$ **b** $\frac{6}{7} \times \frac{7}{6}$ **c** $3 \times \frac{1}{3}$ **d** $\frac{9}{10} \times \frac{10}{9}$

5 Divide these.

  a $\frac{1}{3} \div \frac{1}{3}$ **b** $\frac{1}{4} \div \frac{1}{4}$ **c** $\frac{2}{5} \div \frac{2}{5}$

6 Divide these.

  a $\frac{1}{2} \div \frac{1}{3}$ **b** $\frac{4}{5} \div \frac{1}{10}$ **c** $\frac{7}{8} \div \frac{1}{4}$

  d $\frac{5}{12} \div \frac{5}{9}$ **e** $\frac{3}{4} \div \frac{9}{10}$ **f** $\frac{10}{11} \div \frac{2}{3}$

Reasoning activity

What do you notice about the answers to Question 5?

Did you need to use reciprocals for Question 5? Why or why not?

Dividing fractions

Explain

Fractions can be divided by whole numbers using reciprocals.
Remember that a whole number always has the denominator 1.
So 1 is the same as $\frac{1}{1}$, 2 is the same as $\frac{2}{1}$, 3 is the same as $\frac{3}{1}$.
Dividing a fraction by another number is the same as multiplying the fraction by the reciprocal of the number you wanted to divide by. So we express the whole number as a fraction, then invert it (switch the denominator and numerator) to get the reciprocal, and multiply.

For example: $\frac{1}{2} \div 5 = \frac{1}{2} \div \frac{5}{1} = \frac{1}{2} \times \frac{1}{5} = \frac{1}{10}$

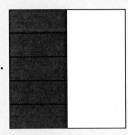

$\frac{1}{2} \div 5 = \frac{1}{10}$

$= \frac{1}{10}$ of the whole.

1 Find the reciprocals of these whole numbers.
   a 3   **b** 11   **c** 5   **d** 144   **e** 18   **f** 1348

2 Express these division problems using the × sign, and then find the answers.
   a $\frac{3}{4} \div 2$ **b** $\frac{7}{8} \div 4$ **c** $\frac{9}{10} \div 3$

   d $\frac{4}{5} \div 10$ **e** $\frac{9}{2} \div 4$

3 Copy and complete these.
   a ___ $\div 6 = \frac{1}{2}$ **b** ___ $\div 9 = \frac{1}{3}$

   c ___ $\div 8 = \frac{3}{4}$ **d** ___ $\div 12 = \frac{2}{3}$

> **Talk about**
> Explain how you found the missing numbers in Question 3.

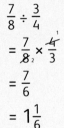

Explain

Fractions can also be divided by proper fractions.
We must invert the proper fractions so that we can work out division problems using reciprocals.

For example: $\frac{15}{12} \div \frac{2}{3}$ Change the operator and $\frac{7}{8} \div \frac{3}{4}$

$= \frac{15}{12} \times \frac{3}{2}$ invert the divisor $= \frac{7}{8} \times \frac{4}{3}$

$= \frac{15}{8}$ $= \frac{7}{6}$

$= 1\frac{7}{8}$ Simplify $= 1\frac{1}{6}$

4 Find the reciprocals of these proper fractions.
   a $\frac{12}{13}$ **b** $\frac{2}{3}$ **c** $\frac{8}{9}$ **d** $\frac{5}{11}$ **e** $\frac{5}{18}$

5 Work out these.
   a $\frac{15}{16} \div \frac{3}{4}$ **b** $\frac{1}{2} \div \frac{8}{9}$ **c** $\frac{15}{25} \div \frac{7}{15}$ **d** $\frac{9}{10} \div \frac{3}{8}$ **e** $\frac{17}{18} \div \frac{1}{3}$

More division of fractions

Explain

Fractions can be divided by mixed numbers. Look at these examples:

$\frac{3}{4} \div 1\frac{1}{8} = \frac{3}{4} \div \frac{9}{8}$ → Change the mixed number to an improper fraction.

$= \frac{\cancel{3}^{1}}{\cancel{4}_{1}} \times \frac{\cancel{8}^{2}}{\cancel{9}_{3}}$ → Change the operator and invert the divisor.

$= \frac{2}{3}$

$1\frac{1}{2} \div 1\frac{5}{6} = \frac{3}{2} \div \frac{11}{6}$ → Change the mixed numbers to improper fractions.

$= \frac{3}{\cancel{2}_{1}} \times \frac{\cancel{6}^{3}}{11}$ → Change the operator and invert the divisor.

$= \frac{9}{11}$

1 Write these mixed numbers as improper fractions.

a $1\frac{11}{12}$ **b** $4\frac{3}{4}$ **c** $9\frac{9}{10}$ **d** $11\frac{10}{11}$ **e** $7\frac{1}{8}$

2 Work out these.

a $\frac{2}{3} \div 2\frac{1}{9}$ **b** $3\frac{1}{5} \div 1\frac{4}{35}$ **c** $2\frac{9}{11} \div 3\frac{1}{2}$ **d** $5\frac{1}{4} \div \frac{7}{8}$

Explain

Sometimes word problems involve fractions. For example:

$\frac{2}{3}$ of the students in a class are boys.

If there are 12 boys in the class, how many students are in the class altogether?

If $\frac{2}{3}$ of the class = 12, then $\frac{1}{3}$ of the class = 12 ÷ 2 = 6

The whole class = ($\frac{1}{3}$ of the class) × 3

= 6 × 3 = 18

There are 18 students in the class.

3 Susan has a bag of apples. $\frac{3}{4}$ of the apples are rotten. If 36 apples are rotten, how many apples does Susan have altogether?

4 In a class, $\frac{3}{4}$ of the students are girls.
There are 28 boys.

a What fraction of the class are boys?

b How many students are in the class?

5 On a BWIA flight, $\frac{2}{3}$ of the passengers are from Trinidad.

If there are 189 passengers altogether, how many are from Trinidad?

Dividing by a fraction

Explain

$\frac{3}{4} \div \frac{7}{16} = ?$

Method 1

Find the LCD, then divide the numerators and denominators.

The LCD of $\frac{3}{4}$ and $\frac{7}{16}$ is 16.

$\frac{3}{4} \times \frac{4}{4} = \frac{12}{16}$

$\frac{12}{16} \div \frac{7}{16} = \frac{12 \div 7}{16 \div 16}$

$\qquad = \frac{12 \div 7}{1}$

$\qquad = \frac{12}{7}$

$\qquad = 1\frac{5}{7}$

Method 2

Multiply $\frac{3}{4}$ by the reciprocal of $\frac{7}{16}$

$\frac{3}{4} \div \frac{7}{16} = \frac{3}{4} \times \frac{16}{7}$ Simplify where possible.

$\qquad = \frac{3}{1} \times \frac{4}{7}$ Multiply.

$\qquad = \frac{12}{7}$

$\qquad = 1\frac{5}{7}$

1 Divide these using the method you find easier.

    a $\frac{6}{7} \div \frac{2}{3}$ **b** $\frac{4}{9} \div \frac{10}{27}$ **c** $\frac{2}{5} \div \frac{3}{15}$ **d** $\frac{12}{13} \div \frac{4}{13}$ **e** $\frac{7}{8} \div \frac{3}{16}$ **f** $\frac{5}{6} \div \frac{3}{15}$

$3 \div \frac{1}{2}$ How many halves are there in three wholes?

Method 1

Find the LCD and divide.

$3 = \frac{3}{1}$

The LCD of $\frac{3}{1}$ and $\frac{1}{2}$ is 2.

$\frac{3}{1} \times \frac{2}{2} = \frac{6}{2}$

$\frac{6}{2} \div \frac{1}{2} = \frac{6 \div 1}{2 \div 2}$

$\qquad = \frac{6}{1}$

$\qquad = 6$

Method 2

Multiply 3 by the reciprocal of $\frac{1}{2}$

$3 = \frac{3}{1}$ Express the whole number as a fraction.

$\frac{3}{1} \div \frac{1}{2} = \frac{3}{1} \times \frac{2}{1}$ Multiply by the reciprocal.

$\qquad = \frac{6}{1}$

$\qquad = 6$

2 Divide these using the method you find easier.

    a $4 \div \frac{1}{3}$ **b** $7 \div \frac{1}{2}$ **c** $2 \div \frac{2}{3}$

    d $8 \div \frac{2}{3}$ **e** $12 \div \frac{2}{4}$ **f** $15 \div \frac{1}{2}$

Reasoning activity

Mark cuts his six patties into thirds so that he can share them with his four friends. He keeps $\frac{1}{9}$ of the pieces for himself and gives $\frac{3}{4}$ of the remaining pieces to his friends. How many pieces does he have left?

Decimals and fractions

Explain

You can express a fraction as a decimal by first converting the denominator to a power of 10.

$\frac{16}{50} = \frac{32}{100} = 0.32$

$2\frac{1}{8} = 2\frac{125}{1000} = 2.125$

You can also express a decimal as a fraction. Count the number of places after the decimal point. That will tell you the number of zeros after the 1 in the denominator. Write the fraction. Then simplify.

$0.4005 = \frac{4\,005}{10\,000} = \frac{801}{2\,000}$

1 Copy the table below. Match each proper fraction from the box with the correct decimal and fill in the pairs in your table.

Fraction	Decimal

$\frac{11}{25}$ 0.9 $\frac{3}{20}$ $\frac{11}{100}$ 12.4

0.875 $\frac{9}{10}$ 0.15 $\frac{6}{15}$

0.008 $12\frac{2}{5}$ 0.4 $\frac{1}{125}$

$\frac{124}{100}$ 0.11   0.44   1.24 $\frac{7}{8}$

2 Maria and Tony are lost in Decimal City. Help them find the path home. Work out whether each statement is true or false. If it is true follow the T path, and if it is false, follow the F path.

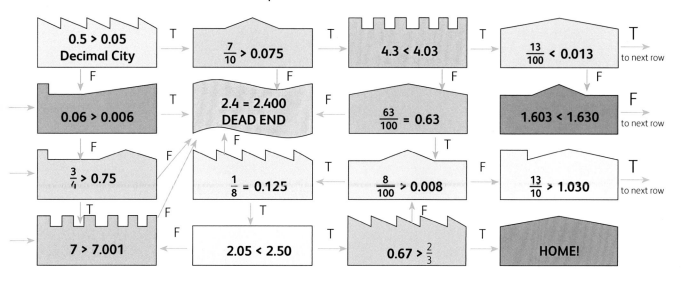

Adding decimals

Explain

When you add decimals, always align the decimal points so that you are adding digits with the same place value. For example:

21.5 + 3.18 + 0.0092

```
  2 1 . 5 0 0 0
    3 . 1 8 0 0
+   0 . 0 0 9 2
───────────────
  2 4 . 6 8 9 2
```

309.57 + 12.346 + 8.0083

```
  3 0 9 . 5 7 0 0
    1 2 . 3 4 6 0
+     8 . 0 0 8 3
─────────────────
  3 2 9 . 9 2 4 3
```

The shaded zeros show the empty decimal places. You can insert these zeros to help you work out the addition.

1 Work out the answer, and then check it using a calculator.

a
```
  3.6
+ 4.2
```

b
```
  5.4
  6.3
+ 9.08
```

c
```
   4.26
  18.1
+ 0.879
```

d
```
   11.20
   15.64
  236.007
+    4
```

2 Work out the answer, and then check it using a calculator.

   a 4.8 + 6.1 **b** 7.5 + 8.46 + 0.9 **c** 2.148 + 4.25 + 17.6 **d** 18.92 + 14.06 + 0.0072

3 At the hardware store, many things are measured in metres and centimetres. Work out the total length of each of the labelled items in the picture.

Subtracting decimals

When you subtract decimals, always align the decimal points of the numbers so that you are subtracting digits with the same place value.
For example:

$$
\begin{array}{r}
37.685 \\
-\ 24.56 \\
\hline
13.125
\end{array}
\qquad
\begin{array}{r}
17.9\overset{8}{\cancel{2}}\overset{11}{\cancel{3}}{}^{1} \\
-\ 16.578 \\
\hline
1.345
\end{array}
\qquad
\begin{array}{r}
\overset{3}{\cancel{4}}.\overset{9}{\cancel{0}}\overset{1}{0} \\
-\ 0.57 \\
\hline
3.43
\end{array}
$$

Subtract these.

1 a
$$
\begin{array}{r}
4.8 \\
-\ 2.6 \\
\hline
\end{array}
$$

b
$$
\begin{array}{r}
14.6 \\
-\ 11.97 \\
\hline
\end{array}
$$

c
$$
\begin{array}{r}
10 \\
-\ 9.7 \\
\hline
\end{array}
$$

d
$$
\begin{array}{r}
13.94 \\
-\ 10.625 \\
\hline
\end{array}
$$

2 Work out these.

a $5.8 - 2.5$ **b** $14.2 - 11.59$ **c** $816.2 - 790.872$

d $12 - 9.148$ **e** $15.4 - 12.8$ **f** $13.5 - 10.41$

3 Work out how much fabric is left on each roll after the pieces in front have been cut off. All the lengths are in metres.

4 The table shows the masses of five children.

What is the difference in mass between:

a Bob and May   **b** Kit and Joan   **c** Paul and May

d Bob and Paul   **e** Bob and Joan   **f** Kit and May?

5 a Between which two children is there the smallest difference in mass?

   b What is the difference in mass?

6 a Between which two children is there the greatest difference in mass?

   b What is the difference in mass?

Child	Mass in kg
May	36.06
Paul	38.11
Kit	41.5
Bob	44
Joan	35.92

Multiplying decimals by powers of 10

1 Choose the right words from the ones in brackets to make each sentence true.

 a When multiplying a decimal by 10, move the digits in the decimal (one place, two places, three places) to the (left, right).

 b When multiplying a decimal by 100, move the digits in the decimal (one place, two places, three places) to the (left, right).

 c When multiplying a decimal by 1000, move the digits in the decimal (one place, two places, three places) to the (left, right).

 d When multiplying a decimal by a power of 10, move the digits in the decimal to the (left, right).
 The number of places = the number of (digits, tens, ones, zeros) in the power of 10.

2 Julie has a bug collection. She lines up her caterpillars.
 Work out how long each line will be if she has 100 of each kind.

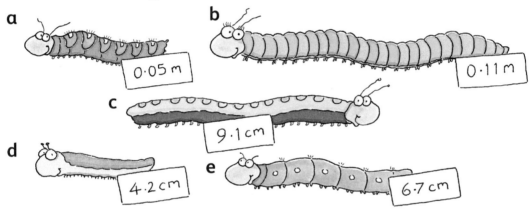

a 0·05 m **b** 0·11 m **c** 9·1 cm **d** 4·2 cm **e** 6·7 cm

3 Work out these.

 a 0.6 × 100 **b** 0.15 × 100 **c** 3.7 × 100 **d** 100 × 0.8 **e** 100 × 0.07

 What do you notice when you multiply by 100?

4 Copy and complete these.

 a 3.4 × 10 = ___   **b** 0.1 × 100 = ___

 c 2.04 × 10 = ___   **d** 20.6 × ___ = 20 600

5 Copy and complete these.

 a ___ × 100 = 520   **b** 0.4 × ___ = 40

 c 0.06 × 1000 = ___   **d** 3.01 × ___ = 3 010

6 a Work out the lengths of these beetles in centimetres.

 b Which type of beetle is the longest?

 c What is the sum of the lengths of the beetles in centimetres?

Beetle type	Length in metres
Blister	0.0148
Colorado	0.0253
Golden	0.0267
Great Water	0.0314
Stag	0.0772

Dividing decimals by powers of 10

1 Choose the right words from the ones in brackets to make each sentence true.

   a When dividing a decimal by 10, move the digits in the decimal
(one place, two places, three places) to the (left, right).

   b When dividing a decimal by 100, move the digits in the decimal
(one place, two places, three places) to the (left, right).

   c When dividing a decimal by 1000, move the digits in the decimal
(one place, two places, three places) to the (left, right).

   d When dividing a decimal by a power of 10, move the digits in the decimal to
the (left, right).
The number of places = the number of (digits, tens, ones, zeros) in the power
of 10.

2 Each coil of rope must be divided into equal lengths.

   a Work out the length of the pieces if each coil is divided into 10 equal pieces.

   b Work out the length of the pieces if each coil is divided into 100 equal pieces.

3·4 m   29.1 m   0·3 m   128 m   5 m

3 Copy and complete these.

   a $2.9 \div \underline{\quad} = 0.29$ **b** $\underline{\quad} \div 1000 = 3.04$ **c** $\underline{\quad} \div 10 = 0.16$

   d $\underline{\quad} \div 10 = 0.69$ **e** $3 \div 100 = \underline{\quad}$ **f** $14 \div 1000 = \underline{\quad}$

4 Work out these.

   a $2.2 \div 10$ **b** $39 \div 10$ **c** $0.9 \div 100$

   d $68 \div 1000$ **e** $950 \div 10\,000$ **f** $1000 \div 10\,000$

5 Work out these.

   a $15.5 \div 10\,000$ **b** $13.398 \div 1000$ **c** $1.11 \div 100$

   d $239.88 \div 10\,000$ **e** $55.476 \div 1000$ **f** $1000 \div 1\,000\,000$

6 Work out the length of each beetle in centimetres.

   a   **b**   **c**   **d**

15.28 mm   16.98 mm   14.67 mm   15.83 mm

Multiplying decimals by whole numbers

Explain

When you multiply a decimal by a whole number, the answer always has the same number of decimal places as the decimal. Always remember to put the decimal point in the correct place in your answer. For example:

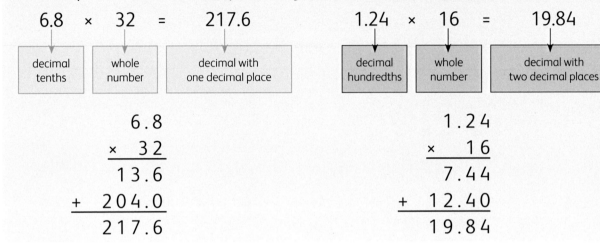

6.8 × 32 = 217.6

| decimal tenths | whole number | decimal with one decimal place |

```
    6.8
×   3 2
  1 3.6
+ 2 0 4.0
  2 1 7.6
```

1.24 × 16 = 19.84

| decimal hundredths | whole number | decimal with two decimal places |

```
    1.2 4
×     1 6
    7.4 4
+ 1 2.4 0
  1 9.8 4
```

1 Multiply these.

   a 1.5 × 14   **b** 14.83 × 15   **c** 1.194 × 22

2 Multiply these.

   a 6.2 × 18   **b** 15.8 × 25   **c** 19.37 × 13

3 Work out these.

0.45 litres

0.225 litres

   a How many litres are there in 6 oil cans?

   b How many litres are there in 25 mugs?

1.575 litres

2.5 litres

   c How many litres are there in 8 buckets?   **d** How many litres are there in 15 kettles?

4 Jenny bought three pieces of ribbon. Each piece was 0.45 metres long. What was the total length of her ribbon?

Multiplying decimals

Explain

When you multiply decimals, the number of decimal places in the product is equal to the sum of the decimal places in the two factors. For example:

0.2	1 decimal place	2.3	1 decimal place

$$
\begin{array}{ll}
0.2 & \text{1 decimal place} \\
\underline{\times\,0.2} & \text{1 decimal place} \\
0.04 & \text{2 decimal places}
\end{array}
\qquad
\begin{array}{ll}
2.3 & \text{1 decimal place} \\
\underline{\times\,0.2} & \text{1 decimal place} \\
0.46 & \text{2 decimal places}
\end{array}
\qquad
\begin{array}{ll}
3.4 & \text{1 decimal place} \\
\underline{\times\,0.24} & \text{2 decimal places} \\
0.816 & \text{3 decimal places}
\end{array}
$$

1 Work out these.

    a 0.9×0.1 **b** 0.3×0.8 **c** 1.2×0.6 **d** 0.05×6 **e** 4×0.9

    f 0.6×5 **g** 0.4×2 **h** 2×0.02 **i** 2.25×0.3 **j** 1.05×0.2

2 Copy these. Put the decimal point in the correct place in each product.

    a $5 \times 0.05 = 25$ **b** $3 \times 2.7 = 81$ **c** $0.9 \times 0.2 = 18$

    d $10.6 \times 0.4 = 424$ **e** $5.2 \times 1.8 = 936$ **f** $6.3 \times 1.2 = 756$

    g $2.3 \times 3.6 = 828$ **h** $10.9 \times 0.5 = 545$ **i** $7.8 \times 0.3 = 234$

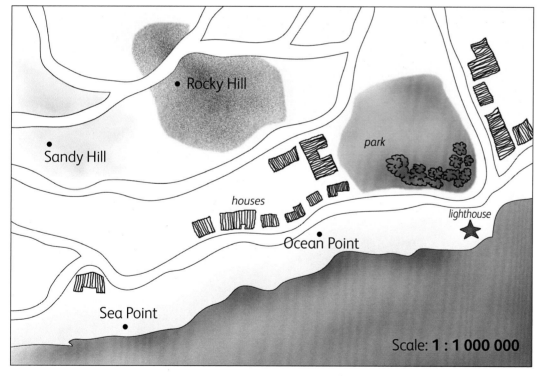

Scale: **1 : 1 000 000**

3 The distance from Ocean Point to Sea Point is 1.5 times the distance from Rocky Hill to Sandy Hill. The distance from Rocky Hill to Sandy Hill is 42.83 km. What is the distance from Ocean Point to Sea Point?

4 Use a ruler to measure these distances in millimetres. Then use the scale to work out the real distances. Express the real distances in km.

    a from Sea Point to Rocky Hill   **b** from Ocean Point to the lighthouse

Dividing decimals by whole numbers

Mr Foster made some toffee.
He divided it into ten equal parts, or
tenths. He cut off $\frac{2}{10}$ or 0.2 of the toffee
for himself. He shared the remaining
$\frac{8}{10}$ or 0.8 of the toffee among his four
children. Each child received $\frac{2}{10}$ or 0.2
of the toffee.

June wrote this sentence and drew a
diagram to explain what her father did:

$0.8 \div 4 = 0.2$

1 Draw a diagram to show each division. Show your working and answers.

  a $0.6 \div 2$ **b** $0.6 \div 3$ **c** $0.8 \div 2$ **d** $0.9 \div 3$ **e** $0.24 \div 6$

  f $0.12 \div 4$ **g** $0.15 \div 5$ **h** $0.36 \div 3$ **i** $0.18 \div 6$ **j** $0.36 \div 4$

2 Copy and complete these. Use your answers to Question 1 to help you.

  a $0.3 \times 2 =$ ___   **b** $0.4 \times$ ___ $= 0.8$ **c** ___ $\times 3 = 0.9$

  d $4 \times$ ___ $= 0.12$ **e** ___ $\times 0.12 = 0.36$ **f** $5 \times$ ___ $= 0.15$

Two men share six tenths of a cake
equally between themselves.
Each receives 0.3 of the cake.

$$\begin{array}{r} 0.3 \\ 2\overline{)0.6} \end{array}$$

3 Work out these.

  a $4\overline{)0.8}$ **b** $5\overline{)0.25}$ **c** $7\overline{)0.42}$ **d** $4\overline{)0.20}$

4 Divide these.

  a $0.24 \div 6$ **b** $15.3 \div 3$ **c** $2.04 \div 3$ **d** $12.16 \div 4$ **e** $9.06 \div 3$

Decimals in long division

```
      3.5      26 goes into 91  3 times.              3.14
26)91           26 × 3 = 78                   14)43.96
  −78           The remainder is 13.              −42
  13.0          Put the decimal point               1.96
 −13.0          after the ones digit.              −1.4
  00.0          0.5 × 26 = 13.0                      0.56
                There is no remainder.             −0.56
                So 91 ÷ 26 = 3.5                     0.00
```

Divide these.
Make sure there are the correct number of decimal places in your answers.

1 a 114 ÷ 5   **b** 11.4 ÷ 5   **c** 1.14 ÷ 5   **d** 907.92 ÷ 12   **e** 9 079.2 ÷ 12
2 a 77.76 ÷ 32   **b** 777.6 ÷ 32   **c** 7.776 ÷ 32   **d** 838.35 ÷ 15   **e** 8 383.5 ÷ 15

3 What number am I? Work out the number for each of the following.
   a If you divide me by 32 you get 3.65.   **b** If you multiply me by 8, you get 11.76.
   c If you multiply me by 9, you get 10.35. **d** I am 5.63 less than one-seventh of 151.34.

4 Each piece of wood must be divided equally into the number of pieces shown
   below it. Work out the length of each piece.

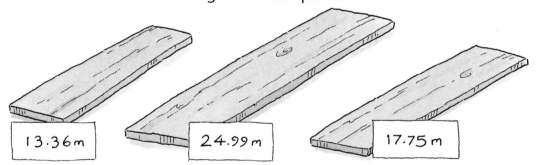

13.36 m   24.99 m   17.75 m

   a 4 equal pieces   **b** 3 equal pieces   **c** 5 equal pieces

5 Each roll of cloth needs to be divided equally into the number of pieces shown
   below it. Work out the length of each piece.

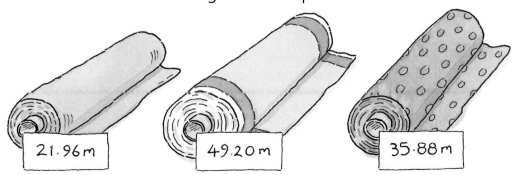

21.96 m   49.20 m   35.88 m

   a 12 equal pieces   **b** 15 equal pieces   **c** 13 equal pieces

Dividing decimals by decimals

Explain

$0.3 \div 0.7 = ?$

Give the answer rounded to three decimal places.

First, convert both decimals to whole numbers.

To do this, multiply them both by 10.

$(0.3 \times 10) \div (0.7 \times 10)$

$= 3 \div 7$ Use long division to find the answer.

$= 0.4285$

0.4285 rounded to three decimal places is 0.429

$$\begin{array}{r} 0.4285 \\ 7\overline{)3.0000} \\ -\,2\,8 \\ \hline 20 \\ -\,1\,4 \\ \hline 60 \\ -\,5\,6 \\ \hline 40 \\ -\,3\,5 \\ \hline 5 \end{array}$$

1 Divide these. Round your answers to three decimal places.

    a $0.5 \div 0.6$ **b** $0.7 \div 0.8$ **c** $0.5 \div 0.7$

    d $0.2 \div 0.9$ **e** $0.6 \div 0.7$ **f** $0.4 \div 0.6$

    g $0.2 \div 0.3$ **h** $0.3 \div 0.7$ **i** $0.8 \div 0.9$

2 Divide these. Round your answers to two decimal places.

    a $0.3 \div 0.8$ **b** $0.4 \div 0.9$ **c** $0.1 \div 0.7$

    d $0.5 \div 0.8$ **e** $0.7 \div 0.4$ **f** $0.3 \div 0.2$

    g $0.1 \div 0.6$ **h** $0.5 \div 0.9$ **i** $0.5 \div 0.6$

Talk about

Why do you think $0.3 \div 0.7$ gives the same answer as $3 \div 7$? (Hint: think about lowest common denominators.)

Explain

Another method for dividing decimals by decimals is to convert the decimals to fractions. For example:

$$0.1 \div 0.3 = \frac{1}{10} \div \frac{3}{10}$$

$$= \frac{1}{\cancel{10}} \times \frac{\cancel{10}}{3}$$

$$= \frac{1}{3}$$

Try this

Work through Question 2 again, this time by converting the decimals to fractions.

Write your answers as proper fractions or mixed numbers. In pairs talk about the different methods for dividing decimals by decimals. Which do you prefer?

Ratio

Ratios

Joe	Jane
○○	○○○

Joe	Jane
XX	**XXX**
XX	**XXX**

These diagrams show how items are shared between Joe and Jane.
The first diagram shows that when Joe gets two, Jane gets three.

The second diagram shows that when Joe gets four, Jane gets six.
The items are still shared in the same **ratio**, 2 for every 3.

1 Draw diagrams to show the following.

   a When Tina gets 2 mangoes, Joseph gets 3 mangoes.

   b When Mike gets 1 ice-cream, Ravi gets 1 ice-cream.

   c For every one marble that Peter gets, Joy gets 2 marbles.
     Peter has 5 marbles. How many marbles does Joy get?

   d For every sweet Indra gets, Suzy gets 3 sweets.
     Indra has 4 sweets. How many sweets does Suzy get?

   e Joan gets 4 hairclips, while her sister gets 2.
     Her sister gets 6 hairclips. How many hairclips does Joan get?

2 Each diagram below shows how a group of shapes was shared.
   Describe the ratio shown in each diagram.

   a 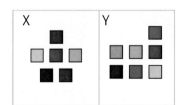   **b** 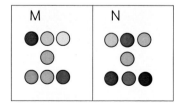   **c**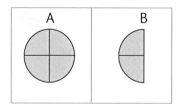

In a youth group, there are three girls for every one boy.

3 How many girls will there be if there are:

   a 2 boys   **b** 4 boys   **c** 6 boys?

4 If there are 15 girls in the group, how many boys are there?

5 How many young people are there altogether if there are 21 girls?

Writing and using ratios

Explain

For every 3 plums that Avril gets, Brian gets 5. If Avril gets 6 plums, then the amount that Brian gets must also double – he will get 10 plums.
We can show this relationship in a table.

Child	Number of plums						
Avril	3	6	9	12	15	18	21
Brian	5	10	15	20	25	30	35

When quantities in the same units are compared like this, they can be expressed as a ratio.
We can say that the ratio of the number of plums that Avril gets to the number that Brian gets is 3 to 5. We can also write this as 3:5.

1 What is being compared in each of these ratios?

a

b

c

Mrs Khundra buys orange squash. It needs to be mixed with water in the ratio 1:4. Notice that there are no units in the ratio itself. This is because the comparison stays the same, no matter what units you use. For example, if Mrs Khundra uses 1 cup of orange squash, she needs 4 cups of water.
The order of the ratio is also important. In this case it is the ratio of squash to water, so the amount of squash must come first. The ratio of water to squash is 4:1.

2 How much water would Mrs Khundra need to add to the following amounts of squash?

a 1 bottle   b 2 cups   c 1 tall glass   d 3 capfuls

3 Look at the shapes in the box.
   Write down the ratio of:

a squares to triangles   b circles to squares

c squares to circles   d triangles to circles.

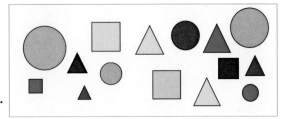

Ratio

3:4 is read as '3 to 4'. So if there are 3 girls for every 4 boys in a class, we could say that the ratio of girls to boys is 3 to 4 or 3:4.

Ratios can be written as fractions if they are being compared to the whole amount. The ratio of girls to the whole class is 3 to 7 or 3:7.

This means we can also say that $\frac{3}{7}$ of the class are girls and $\frac{4}{7}$ are boys.

If $\frac{3}{4}$ of your class are right-handed, we could say that 3 out of every 4 children are right-handed and 1 out of every 4 is left-handed.

This means that the ratio of right-handed to left-handed is 3:1.

1 In the boxes, you can see how boys and girls are matched in groups – there are 2 girls for every 1 boy.

How many girls will be matched with:

a 2 boys   b 4 boys   c 6 boys?

d If there are 10 girls, how many boys will there be?

e How many boys would be matched with 14 girls?

2 Joan and Derrick shared $24. This is how they shared their money.

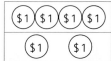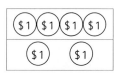

Joan

Derrick

a How much did Joan get?   b How much did Derrick get?

c What is the ratio of Joan's money to Derrick's money?

d What fraction of the whole amount did Joan receive?

e If Joan got $40, how much would Derrick get if the money was shared in the same ratio?

f If Derrick get $16, how much would Joan get if the money was shared in the same ratio?

Reasoning activity

They received a sum of money and it was shared in the ratio of 2:3. Derrick got $18 more than Joan.

a How much money did they receive in total?

b How much did Joan get?

c How much did Derrick get?

Comparing using ratios

1 Write the ratio of red parts to blue parts in each shape.

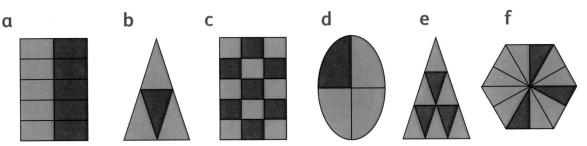

a   b   c   d   e   f

2 Look at the shapes again.
This time write the ratio of blue parts to red parts in each shape.

3 Write these as ratios.

   a 12 cm to 25 cm   **b** 100 km to 250 km   **c** $45 to $90   **d** 3 goals to 5 goals

Explain

Remember: Ratios can be used to compare quantities only when they are expressed in the same units. For example:
The ratio of 25c to $1 is 25 : 100.
To work out the ratio we change both amounts to the same units – cents.

4 Change these amounts to the same units. Write each comparison as a ratio.

   a 50 cents to $250   **b** 2 years to 18 months

   c 1 cm to 230 mm   **d** 20 minutes to 1 hour

5 Write each sentence as a ratio.

   a In Jamaica there is one teacher for every 45 students.

   b To cook rice you use 3 cups of water for every cup of rice.

   c Sara is twice as tall as her baby sister.

Reasoning activity

Mrs Adams likes to place bets on horse races. The betting on a race is shown on the poster. 5 : 1 means that for every $1 you bet on a horse, you will be paid $5 if that horse wins. Mrs Adams bets $1000 on each horse.
How much will she win if:

   a Salsa wins the race   **b** Sweetmoney wins the race

   c Bajan King wins the race?

   d How much will she lose if none of these three horses wins?

<u>Race 7</u>
Salsa   5 :
Sweetmoney 7 :
Bajan King   7 :

Equivalent ratios

Explain

Ratios behave in a similar way to fractions.

$\frac{1}{2} = \frac{2}{4} = \frac{3}{6} = \frac{4}{8}$ and so on. $\frac{1}{2}, \frac{2}{4}, \frac{3}{6}$ and $\frac{4}{8}$ are equivalent fractions.

In the same way, the ratio $3:5 = 6:10 = 9:15 = 12:20$ and so on.

These are called **equivalent ratios**.

We can use equivalent ratios to solve problems.

For example:

Cathy and Stella share mangoes in the ratio $5:4$.

If Cathy gets 20 mangoes, how many does Stella get?

Use a table to show the increasing ratios.

Cathy	5	10	15	20
Stella	4	8	12	16

This shows that when Cathy gets 20, Stella gets 16.

The table also shows that $5:4 = 20:16$.

1 Copy and complete the equivalent ratios.

   a $1:2 = 4:$ ____

   b $3:5 =$ ____ $:15$

   c $1:5 = 5:$ ____

   d $3:4 =$ ____ $:20$

   e $16:8 =$ ____ $:1$

   f $30:12 = 5:$ ____

Explain

Like fractions, ratios are usually written in their simplest form. To write a ratio in its simplest form you divide both terms of the ratio by the highest common factor. For example:

$12:4$ is not in its simplest form. The highest common factor of 12 and 4 is 4.

$12:4 = \frac{12}{4} : \frac{4}{4} = 3:1$

2 Write these ratios in their simplest form.

   a $4:2$ **b** $5:15$ **c** $2:8$

   d $20:10$ **e** $12:3$ **f** $4:20$

3 Simplify each ratio.

   a $10:100$ **b** $12:24$ **c** $16:48$

   d $99:45$ **e** $2:4:6$ **f** $4:12:36$

   g $2:50$ **h** $12:30$ **i** $9:63$

   j $86:86$ **k** $3:9:30$ **l** $10:100:50$

Try this

Use sets of object to help demonstrate equivalent ratios. For example, make a group of 4 blue counters and 6 red counters. Show how we can divide both parts in two, to make two groups of 2 blue : 3 red counters.

More ratios

1 There are 3 girls for every 2 boys at a party.

   a Draw boxes to show the ratio of boys to girls.

   b There are 20 boys at the party. How many girls are there?

2 A recipe for 20 muffins uses 2 eggs. How many eggs are needed for:

   a 40 muffins   **b** 10 muffins   **c** 50 muffins?

3 Pam ate 9 nuts in 6 minutes.
   If she continued eating at the same rate, how many nuts would she eat in:

   a 12 minutes   **b** 4 minutes   **c** 1 hour?

4 It takes a carpenter 5 days to build 8 tables.
   If the carpenter continues working at the same rate, work out:

   a how many tables can be built in 20 days

   b how many days it takes to build 24 tables.

5 Answer these problems.

   a A man makes 10 fish pots in a day.
   How long will he take to make 35 fish pots if he continues at the same rate?

   b In two days, a seamstress sews 9 dresses.
   How many days will she take to sew 36 dresses if she continues at the same
   rate?

6 Look at the picture and
   answer these.

   a How many water glasses
   could you buy for
   $1000.00?

   b The shopkeeper has
   75 large teapots and
   45 small teapots in stock.
   What is the ratio of large
   teapots to small teapots?

Cooking sets: include frying pan, saucepan and cooking pan, with soup pot and small pot. All for $2000.00!

Special: $300.00 for four water glasses!

Special: buy 3 bowls, get 2 cups!

   c A restaurant owner
   bought 18 bowls. How
   many free cups did he receive?

   d What is the ratio of pans to pots in each cooking set?

Calculating ratios

1 Jill and Sarah are carrying newspapers from their classroom to the recycling depot. There are 20 bundles of newspapers in the classroom.
On each trip, Jill carries 3 bundles and Sarah carries 2 bundles.

   a How many trips do the girls make to carry all 20 bundles to the depot?

   b How many bundles of newspaper does each girl carry in total?

2 Jill's class also collects old magazines to take to the nearby hospital.
For every 2 magazines that go into the small collection box, 4 magazines go into the big collection box. One week, the children collect 210 magazines.

   a Draw a diagram to show how the magazines are shared between the collection boxes.

   b How many magazines go into each box?

3 Jennifer and Sam went picking mangoes.
Jennifer could pick 11 mangoes in the time that Sam took to pick 7 mangoes.
When they went home, they had a total of 36 mangoes.
How many mangoes did they each pick?

4 Paula and Jonathan shared 51 mangoes. Paula got twice as many as Jonathan.

   a Draw boxes to show each child's share.

   b What was Paula's share?

   c What was Jonathan's share?

Using ratios in enlargement

Explain

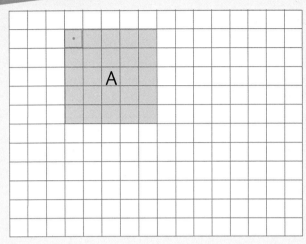 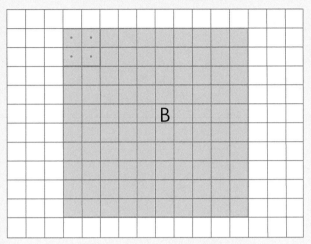

The sides of square A have been enlarged using a ratio of 2:1 to draw square B.
The area of square B has 4 units for every 1 unit of the area of square A.

A ratio can also be expressed as a percentage. $4:1 = \frac{4}{1} = \frac{400}{100} = 400\%$

If square A represents 100%, square B represents 400%.

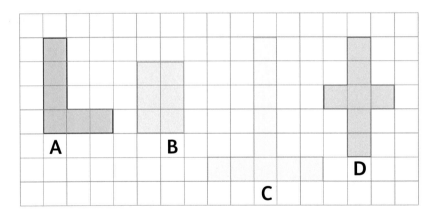

1 Use a pencil, ruler and centimetre squared paper for these activities.

   a Enlarge shape A using a ratio of 4:1.
   (Use 4 blocks for every 1 block in the original shape.)

   b Draw shape B using a ratio of 2:1 for the sides.

   c Draw shape C. Make your shape half the size of the original.
   Write the ratio under your drawing.

   d Draw shape D so that it represents 300% of the original.

Rates

Explain

A **rate** compares quantities measured using two different units.
Examples of rates are:

- speed, such as kilometres per hour or metres per second
- wages and salaries, such as dollars per month or dollars per hour
- prices, such as dollars per kilogram.

For example:

Apples are being sold for $50 per kilogram.
How much would it cost to buy:

1 kg costs $50.

- 2 kg
- 10 kg
- $\frac{1}{2}$ kg?

When we calculate rates, we multiply or divide both sides by the same amount.

2 kg cost ☐ ?

$50 × 2 = $100

2 kg of apples cost $100.

$50 × 10 = $500

10 kg of apples cost $500.

$\frac{1}{2}$ of $50 = $25

$\frac{1}{2}$ kg of apples cost $25.

Janet travels at 60 km per hour.

1 How far does she travel in:

   a 1 hour   **b** 2 hours   **c** 3 hours   **d** 5 hours   **e** $\frac{1}{2}$ hour   **f** $\frac{1}{4}$ hour?

2 How long does it take her to travel:

   a 240 km   **b** 600 km   **c** 90 km?

3 Ben earns $25 000.00 per day working part-time.
   How much does he earn in:

   a 3 days   **b** 10 days?

   c How many days would he have to work to earn
   $500 000.00?

Look at the picture on the right.

4 What is the rate that describes the price of
   gasoline?

5 If my tank takes 60 litres, how much would it
   cost to fill:

   a the whole tank   **b** $\frac{1}{2}$ tank   **c** $\frac{1}{4}$ tank?

Talk about

Look at a newspaper.
Find examples of five
different rates and
discuss what they
are used for.

Gasoline
$130 per litre

Solving problems using ratios

1 This plan of a classroom has been drawn in the ratio 1:100. This means that every 1 cm on the plan is equivalent to 100 cm in the real classroom.

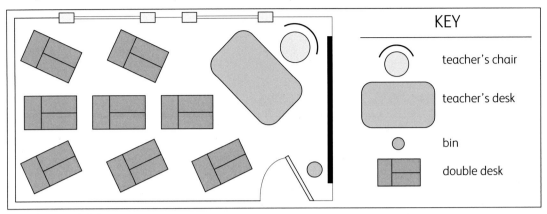

KEY

teacher's chair

teacher's desk

bin

double desk

Scale 1:100

a How wide is the classroom on the plan? How wide is the real classroom?

b How long is the teacher's desk?

c How long is one student's desk?

2 What is the actual length of each animal?

a

b

1:4

1:5

3 The ratio of girls to boys at St Stephen's Primary School is 5:4. If there are 630 students, how many are girls?

4 Write each of these sentences as a ratio.

a There is 1 teacher for every 45 students.

b To cook rice and peas, you use 4 cups of water for every cup of rice and peas.

c Zahra is twice as tall as her little brother.

d A dog weighs 4 times as much as a cat.

12 Percentage

Percentages

A **percentage** is like a fraction with a denominator of 100. We write percentages with a special sign, %. We use percentages in many real-life situations.

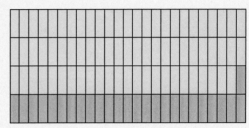

71% of the Earth's surface is covered by oceans. Another 3% is covered by rivers and lakes. The rest is land.

We can show these percentages on a rectangle divided into 100 parts. $\frac{1}{100}$ is the same as 1 per cent = 1%.

Remember that the whole amount is always 100%.
Any part of the whole is a percentage of the whole.

1 What do these mean?
  a 5 per cent   b 80 per cent   c 15 per cent   d 100 per cent

2 Write each of these using the % symbol.
  a 5 per cent   b 90 per cent   c 100 per cent   d $12\frac{1}{2}$ per cent

3 3% can also be written as $\frac{3}{100}$. Write these percentages as fractions.
  a 5%   b 10%   c 15%   d 25%   e 40%

4 Study the diagrams. Write down what percentage of each diagram is coloured red, blue, yellow and orange.

a 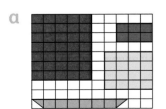   b 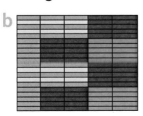   c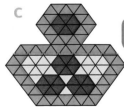

Remember

Express percentages as fractions out of 100.

Percentages, fractions and decimals

To convert a fraction to a percentage, rewrite the fraction with a denominator of 100. For example:

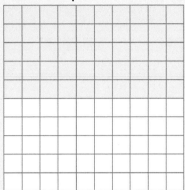

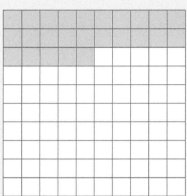

$\frac{1}{2} = \frac{50}{100} = 50$ out of 100

$\frac{1}{2} = 50\%$

$\frac{1}{4} = \frac{25}{100} = 25$ out of 100

$\frac{1}{4} = 25\%$

$\frac{1}{6}$ as a percentage $= \frac{1}{6} \times 100 = \frac{100}{6} = \frac{50}{3} = 16\frac{2}{3}$

$\frac{1}{6} = 16\frac{2}{3}\%$

1 Copy these. Draw diagrams to help you complete them.

   a $\frac{3}{4} = \frac{\square}{100} = $ ___ %
   b $1 = \frac{\square}{100} = $ ___ %
   c $1\frac{1}{2} = \frac{\square}{100} = $ ___ %

2 Copy and complete these.

   a $\frac{1}{5} = \frac{\square}{100} = $ ___ %
   b $\frac{3}{5} = \frac{\square}{100} = $ ___ %
   c $\frac{7}{10} = \frac{\square}{100} = $ ___ %

   d $\frac{13}{50} = \frac{\square}{100} = $ ___
   e $\frac{5}{25} = \frac{\square}{100} = $ ___ %
   f $\frac{3}{20} = \frac{\square}{100} = $ ___ %

3 Write each fraction as a percentage.

   a $\frac{20}{100}$
   b $\frac{8}{10}$
   c $\frac{6}{24}$
   d $\frac{7}{50}$
   e $\frac{3}{5}$
   f $\frac{9}{20}$
   g $\frac{1}{7}$
   h $\frac{5}{8}$

4 What percentage of each diagram is shaded?

   a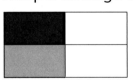
   b
   c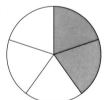

Reasoning activity

$\frac{1}{2}$ of A = B

25 % of B = C

If A = 72 what is the value of C?

Decimals and percentages

Explain

$0.28 = \frac{28}{100} = 28\%$ $1.6 = \frac{16}{10} = \frac{160}{100} = 160\%$ $45\% = \frac{45}{100} = 0.45$
or $45 \div 100 = 0.45$

$13\frac{1}{2}\% = 13.5 \div 100 = 0.135$ $0.02 = \frac{2}{100} = 2\%$

Write these percentages as decimals.

1 a 12%   b 98%   c 2%   d 80%   e 7%   f 100%

2 a $9\frac{9}{10}\%$ b $95\frac{1}{3}\%$ c $5\frac{1}{8}\%$ d $52\frac{3}{5}\%$ e $8\frac{5}{6}\%$

3 a 18.2%   b 6.5%   c 25.25%   d 80.75%   e 99.05%

Write these decimals as percentages.

4 a 0.13   b 0.09   c 0.56   d 0.20   e 0.50   f 0.99

5 a 0.1   b 0.6   c 0.9   d 0.3   e 0.25   f 0.75

6 a 0.44   b 0.02   c 0.22   d 0.01   e 0.04   f 0.14

7 a 0.4   b 0.31   c 0.18   d 0.45   e 0.05   f 0.08

8 Study the diagram, and then copy and complete the table.

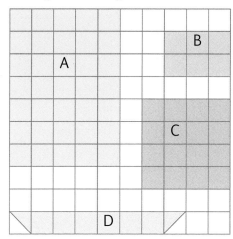

Part of diagram shaded	Fraction	Decimal	Percentage
A			
B			
C			
D			

Reasoning activity

25% of P = Q
$\frac{1}{5}$ of Q = R
10% of R = 0.7
P + Q + R = ____

Percentages of quantities

Explain

Per cent means 'out of a hundred'.

3% means 3 out of every hundred.

So 3% of 200 is $\frac{3}{100} \times \frac{200}{1} = \frac{600}{100} = 6$.

Since 3% is 3 out of every hundred, then out of 200 it would be 6.

1 Find:

    a 2% of 200   b 20% of 600   c 50% of 40   d 10% of 80

    e 75% of 50   f 5% of 60   g 100% of 40   h 15% of 90

2 A shoe shop has a sale and reduces all its prices by 20%.
Copy and complete the table by filling in the original price and the sale price.

Item	Original price	20% of original price	Sale price
ladies' shoes		$360	
gents' shoes		$440	
boys' sandals		$400	

3 A carpenter has to increase his prices by 15% because the cost of wood has risen. Work out what the new price of each item will be.

$7000

$2500

$24000

Talk about

How is land used in your parish? What do you think the biggest percentage is used for? Why?

4 The area of Jamaica is approximately 11 400 km². Copy and complete the table to show how much land is used for various types of agriculture.

Land use	Percentage	Area in km²
crops	17	
permanent pasture	41	
forest and woodland	20	
other	22	2 508

Try this

Think of examples of real-life percentages – for example: what is 50% of your class (half the number of students in the class)?

Calculating percentages

Explain

Remember, 'per cent' means 'out of 100'. So 3 per cent means 3 out of every 100, and is the same as $\frac{3}{100}$. So 3% of 60 = $\frac{3}{100} \times \frac{60}{1} = \frac{18}{10} = 1\frac{4}{5}$.

We can also work out the total amount if we have a percentage.

For example: If 60 represents 15%, then 1% is $\frac{60}{15}$ = 4

So 100% is 100 x 4 = 400.

1   Work out these. Write your answers as whole numbers or mixed numbers.

    a 2% of 200   b 10% of 600   c 50% of 175   d 20% of 80

    e 75% of 50   f 5% of 40   g 100% of 72   h 15% of 55

2   Now write your answers to Question 1 as decimals.
    Use your calculator to check your answers.

3   Work out these. Write your answers as decimals. Show your working.

    a 10% of 85   b 5% of 171   c 15% of 90

    d 20% of 16   e 15% of 300   f 75% of 145

4   In a school of 400 students, 30% are boys.

    a How many boys are there?   b How many girls are there?

5   A fish weighed 6.4 kg. A fishmonger dried it, and it lost 25% of its weight.
    How many kilograms did the fish lose through drying?

6   Copy and complete these.

    a 15 is ___% of 30   b 40 is ___% of 80   c 15 is ___% of 45

    d ___% of 50 = 10   e ___% of 80 = 36   f ___% of 120 = 60

7   a What percentage of 50 is 20?   b What percentage of 150 is 90?

8   After travelling 40 km, a motorist still has 60% of the journey to travel.
    What is the total length of the journey?

9   a 50% of a number is 25. What is the number?

    b 45% of a number is 45. What is the number?

    c 80% of John's salary is $180 000. What is his salary?

10 a Jeremy scored 60% of the total marks on a test. If
    the test was marked out of 75, what was his score?

    b Sammy was given 75% of a sum of money.
    If Sammy received $120, what was the total sum
    of money?

Ratios and percentages

Explain

We can work with ratios in the same way as we work with fractions.
For example:
$4 : 5 = ? : 100$
Find an equivalent fraction using 100 as the denominator.
$\frac{4}{5} = \frac{?}{100}$ $\frac{4}{5} \times \frac{20}{20} = \frac{80}{100}$
So $4 : 5 = 80 : 100$

1 Write each ratio as a fraction, then find the equivalent fraction using
   a denominator of 100.

a 2:5	b 3:4	c 1:2	d 7:10	e 4:1
f 7:20	g 4:25	h 13:50	i 9:20	j 17:5

Explain

We can convert ratios and fractions into percentages.
100 passengers travelled on an aeroplane to Montego Bay.
Each passenger could choose jerk chicken or jerk fish for their meal.
Two out of five passengers chose fish.
What percentage of the passengers ate fish, and what percentage ate chicken?
For every 5 passengers, 2 ate fish and 3 ate chicken.
So $\frac{2}{5}$ of the passengers ate fish and $\frac{3}{5}$ ate chicken.
Now convert these fractions to fractions out of 100.
$\frac{2}{5} \times \frac{20}{20} = \frac{40}{100}$ $\frac{3}{5} \times \frac{20}{20} = \frac{60}{100}$
40 % of the passengers ate fish and 60 % ate chicken.

2 88 people went to the beach.
   One in four people hired an umbrella.
   a What percentage of the people hired umbrellas?
   b How many people hired umbrellas and how many
      didn't?
   c If the umbrella vendor charged $200 per umbrella,
      how much money did he make that day?

3 280 people watched a play. One out of every seven people bought a programme.
   a What percentage of the audience bought programmes?
   b How many people bought programmes and how many didn't?
   c If the programmes cost $120 each, how much money did the programme
      vendor make that day?

Ratios, fractions and percentages

Remember, just as we have equivalent fractions, we also have equivalent ratios.

$\frac{3}{4} = \frac{6}{8} = \frac{9}{12} = \frac{12}{16}$ **OR** $3:4 = 6:8 = 9:12 = 12:16$

1 Write five equivalent ratios for each of the following.

   a 2:5   b 1:2   c 4:7   d 7:8   e 4:5

2 Copy and complete these.

   a 11:12 = ___ :36   b ___ :3 = 10:15   c 9:11 = ___ :33   d 7:8 = ___ :56

3 Copy and complete these. Write the ratio in its simplest form.

   a 5:15 = ___:___   b 8:12 = ___:___   c 4:16 = ___:___

   d 18:24 = ___ :12 = ___:___   e 24:36 = ___:___ = 2: ___

4 You can increase or enlarge the size of a picture
   using a photocopier. Most photocopiers can be set
   to reduce or enlarge by a percentage.
   Maria has copied a page at 75%.
   This means her copy is 75% or $\frac{3}{4}$ of the original size,
   so the ratio of the copy to the original size is 3:4.
   What is the ratio of the copy to the original size
   when you reduce by:

   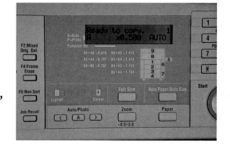

   a 50%   b 20%   c 80%?

Reasoning activity

What happens to the area shown on the map as the scale decreases?
Discuss this in groups and explain your reasoning.

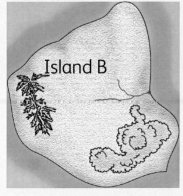

1:150 000

1:300 000

1:600 000

13 Problem solving using percentage and ratio

Solving percentage problems

1 Garry keeps birds in a cage. He has 27 green parrots, 15 ground doves and 8 red-necked pigeons.

  a What percentage of the birds in the cage are parrots?

  b What percentage of his birds are red-necked pigeons?

2 Mrs Sinclair has 280 chocolates. She gives 40% of the chocolates to Tommy, 30% to Andrew, 20% to Samantha and 10% to Christiana.
How many chocolates does each student get?

3 In Jamaica, 20 000 workers were employed by the bauxite industry. One plant closed down and 15% of the workers had to be moved to other industries.
How many workers were moved?

4 A box contained 120 oranges. 20% of them were not suitable for sale.

  a How many oranges were unsuitable for sale?

  b How many oranges could be sold?

5 A chair was priced at $80. The price was increased by 25%.
What was the new price?

6 James gave $\frac{1}{5}$ of a cake to Sid and $\frac{2}{5}$ to Kim.

  a What percentage of the cake did he give away?

  b What percentage of the cake did he have left?

7 Zayn cut 30% off a plank that was 3 metres long.
How many centimetres did he cut off?

8 The customs duty on imported cars is 25%.
How much duty would you pay to import a car that cost US$10 000?

Talk about

Look at the picture.

20% off

BANK
We pay
10%
interest

Where else do you use percentages in your daily life?

Remember

It can be helpful to express a problem as a number sentence before you try to solve it.

Problems involving percentages

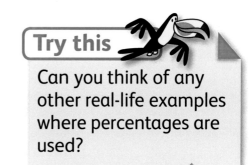

Try this

Can you think of any other real-life examples where percentages are used?

1 Copy and complete this table.

Item	Original price	Reduction of 20%	Sale price
1 pair of ladies' shoes	$800.00		
1 pair of gents' shoes			
1 pair of boys' shoes			

2 The cost of wood went up and a carpenter had to increase the price of her furniture by 15%. The picture shows the old prices.
Work out the new prices, then copy and complete the table.

Item	Original price	Increase of 15%	New price
large table	$8000.00		
set of chairs	$6500.00		
small table	$3500.00		

Reasoning activity

5% of a number is 15. Work out:
a 50% of the number   b 98% of the number   c 2% of the number.
In small groups explain your methods for solving these. Are some methods more efficient than others? Why?

14 Area

Tessellation

Tessellation is the tiling of a flat surface using geometric shapes.

We use tiling to cover floors, walls and other surfaces.

Tiling is also a way to create patterns.

1 What shapes have been used in the following tessellations?

a

b

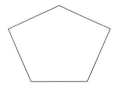

c

2 a Choose any of the shapes below. Trace and cut out copies of the shape. Use your cut-outs to tile a piece of legal size paper.

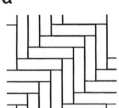

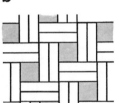

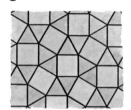

b Seal your tiled pattern with adhesive plasic (contact paper) to make a useful placemat!

Talk about

How do we use tiling and tessellation in daily life? Think of surfaces outside and inside your home and other buildings. Describe as many examples as you can.

Remember

When shapes fit together in a regular pattern, with no gaps between them, we say that they tessellate.

Units of area

Explain

The **area** of a shape is the amount of surface it covers.
We measure area in square units, such as:

- square centimetres (cm²)
- square metres (m²)
- square kilometres (km²).

We use smaller units to measure smaller surfaces
and larger units to measure larger surfaces.

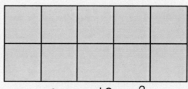

Area = 10 cm²

1 Say which unit should be used to measure each area.

  a a page of your exercise book   **b** a parish

  c your school grounds   **d** the national stadium

  e a race track   **f** your classroom

  g the door to the principal's office   **h** the teacher's desk

  i the set square in your geometry set

Explain

To calculate the area of a rectangle, we multiply length by width.

For example: 3 cm × 2 cm = 6 cm²

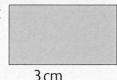

The area of the rectangle is 6 cm².

2 Trace these rectangles. Place them on centimetre squared paper.

  a   **b**   **c**

3 Copy and complete this
table for the rectangles
in Question 2.

	Length	Width	Length × width	Area
a				
b				
c				

Areas of squares

1 Copy this and complete it. The area of a square = ＿＿ × ＿＿

2 Calculate the area of the following squares.

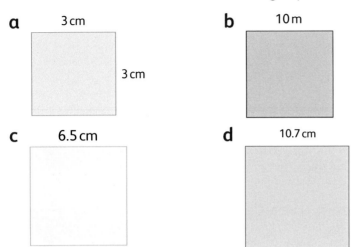

a 3 cm, 3 cm

b 10 m

c 6.5 cm

d 10.7 cm

3 A square plot of land is 14 metres long. Find its area.

4 The side of a square discount stamp is 4.1 cm.

   a Find its area in square millimetres.

   b A sheet of discount stamps has six rows of stamps, with five stamps in a row.
Find the area of a sheet of discount stamps if there are no spaces between the stamps.

   c Find the area of the remaining sheet if one row has been torn off.

5 A rug covers a square floor exactly. The length of one side of the floor is 8.2 metres. Calculate the area of the rug in square metres.

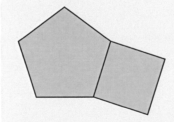

Reasoning activity

This shape is made from a regular pentagon and a square.

The area of the square is 81 cm². What is the perimeter of the whole shape?

More areas of squares

1 The area of a square is 81 mm². What is the length of one side?

2 The length of one side of a square is 5.5 cm. Find the perimeter and the area.

3 The perimeter of a square lawn is 120 metres. Find its area.

4 Mr Martin had 200 metres of fencing wire.
He used all of it to fence a square garden.

   a What is the length of one side of the garden?

   b What is the area of the garden?

5 A piece of rope 64 cm long is formed into a
square.

   a Find the length of a side of the square.

   b Find the area of the square.

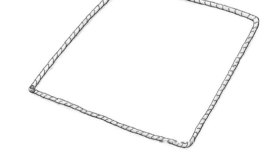

Try this

Can you come up with other ways to find the
area of squares?

Areas of squares and rectangles

1 Find the area of each rectangle.

a 5 cm
3 cm

b 9 cm
4 cm

c 12 cm
3 cm

2 Find the area of each rectangle.

a length 6 cm, width 4 cm

b length 9.2 cm, width 6 cm

c length 8.5 cm, width 7.3 cm

3 What is the area of a rectangle that measures 9 cm by 81 mm?

4 Work out the length of the missing side for each rectangle.

a area = 12 cm²
length = 6 cm,
width = _____

b area = 23.2 cm²
length = 8 cm,
width = _____

c area = 39 cm²
length = _____,
width = 6 cm

d area = 42 cm²
length = _____,
width = 60 mm

Explain

You can use the areas of squares and rectangles to work out the area of other shapes. For example:
Area of large rectangle = 10 cm × 8 cm = 80 cm²
Area of shaded rectangle = 7 cm × 3 cm = 21 cm²
Area of unshaded part = 80 cm² − 21 cm²
= 59 cm²

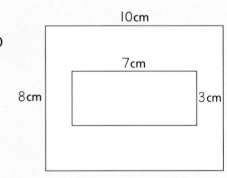

5 Calculate the area of the unshaded part of each shape.

a
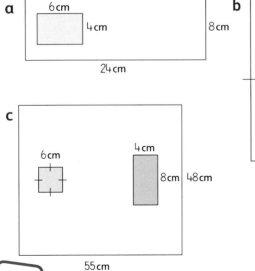

6 cm
4 cm
8 cm
24 cm

b
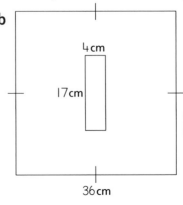

4 cm
17 cm
36 cm

c
6 cm
4 cm
8 cm 48 cm
55 cm

Try this

Can you think of ways to calculate the area of shapes made up of squares and rectangles?

Areas of triangles

A triangle is a shape that has three straight sides and three interior angles. There is a special formula for working out the area of a triangle.

Look at the grid. What is the area of rectangle ABCD?

Length = 4 cm, width = 3 cm

Area = 4 cm × 3 cm = 12 cm²

The triangle BCD takes up half the space (area) of the rectangle.

$\frac{1}{2}$ × (3 cm × 4 cm) = $\frac{1}{2}$ × 12 cm²

           = 6 cm²

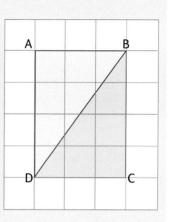

1 For each of the following, use your ruler to measure the sides. Find the area of the rectangle, the area of half the rectangle, and the area of the shaded triangle.

a   **b**   **c**   **d**

2 Find the area of each triangle.

a
40 mm
20 mm

b
4 cm
5 cm

c
3 cm
4 cm
5 cm

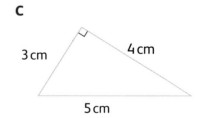

3 Find the area of the following shapes.

a
12 cm
7 cm

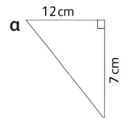

b
3.4 cm
8.2 cm

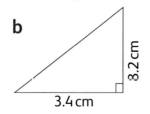

c
9 cm
9 cm
15.6 cm

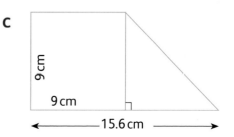

More about areas of triangles

Explain

Find the areas of triangles ABD and BDC.

Both triangles are right-angled triangles created by the diagonal DB.

Area of rectangle = length × width

$$= 10 \text{ cm} × 8 \text{ cm}$$

$$= 80 \text{ cm}^2$$

The length of the rectangle also forms the base of each triangle.

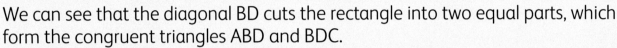

We can see that the diagonal BD cuts the rectangle into two equal parts, which form the congruent triangles ABD and BDC.

The area of each triangle = $\frac{1}{2}$ the area of the rectangle

$$= 40 \text{ cm}^2$$

Another way to express this is:

Area of triangle = $\frac{1}{2}$ (base × height).

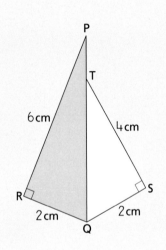

Find the area of this shape.

Area of triangle PQR = $\frac{1}{2}$ (base × height)

$$= \frac{1}{2} (2 \text{ cm} × 6 \text{ cm})$$

$$= 6 \text{ cm}^2$$

Area of triangle TSQ = $\frac{1}{2}$ (2 cm × 4 cm)

$$= 4 \text{ cm}^2$$

Area of PTSQR = 6 cm² + 4 cm² = 10 cm²

1 Find the area of each shape.

a

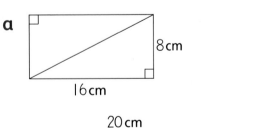

b

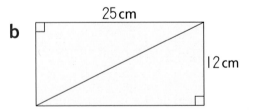

c

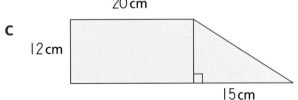

d

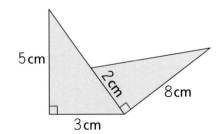

Solving problems involving perimeter and area

1 Find the area of each rectangle.

a
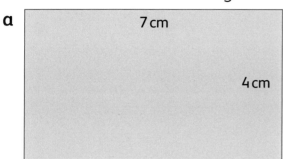
7 cm

4 cm

b
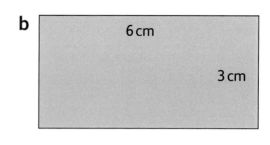
6 cm

3 cm

2 If the width of a rectangular floor is 4 metres and the area is 31 m², what is the length?

3 The area of a rectangle is 120 cm². The width is 10 cm.

a Find the length.

b Find the perimeter.

4 The two lengths of a rectangle together measure 20 cm. The width is 8 cm. What is the area of the rectangle?

5 The length of a patch of land is twice its width. The width is 6 metres. What is the area of the patch of land?

6 The width of this rectangle is half its length. The length is 19 metres.

a What is the perimeter of the rectangle?

b What is the area of the rectangle?

19 m
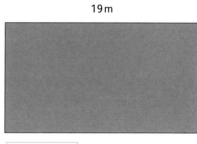

7 This is the floor plan of a room. It has been drawn so that 1 cm represents 6 metres in the actual room.

Find:

a the length of the room

b the width of the room

c the area of the floor.

Reasoning activity

This shape is made from two different sized rectangles.

60 m
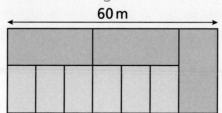

For each large rectangle the length is double the width.
What is the area of one of the small rectangles?

Areas of irregular shapes

Look at this shape. It does not have a regular shape like a square, rectangle or triangle. How can we find the area of this **irregular** shape?

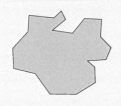

We can use the blocks to help us estimate the area of the shape.

Each block = 1 cm².

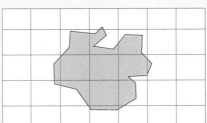

Count all the blocks covered by the shape. For each blocks that is partly covered, estimate what fraction of the block is covered (for example, $\frac{5}{6}$ or $\frac{1}{10}$).

Add all the fractions and whole numbers together and estimate the area.

1 Estimate the area of each shaded shape by counting the covered squares and fractions of squares.

a

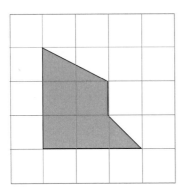

b

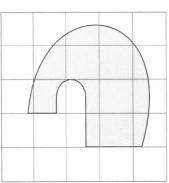

c

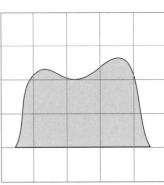

2 On a piece of paper, draw the perimeter of your friend's hand and your own hand. On another piece, draw the perimeter of your friend's foot and your own foot. Estimate the areas and compare. Whose hand and foot takes up a larger area?

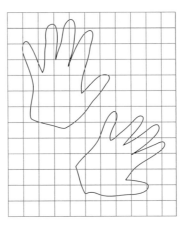

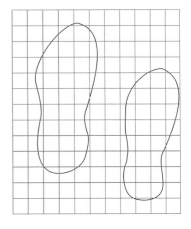

Areas of parallelograms

Explain

You already know that a parallelogram is a 2-D shape that has two pairs of opposite sides that are parallel and equal in length.

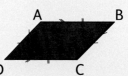

We write: AB = CD and AD = BC

AB ∥ CD and AD ∥ BC

We can use blocks to help us to find the area of a parallelogram by drawing it on squared paper. Each block represents 1 cm².

Count all the blocks covered by the parallelogram (6 whole squares and 4 half squares).

The area of the parallelogram is 8 cm².

Another way is to split the parallelogram up into triangles and rectangles.

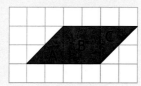

Can you see that the area of triangles A and C are each equal to 2 cm², and the area of the square B is 4 cm²?

2 + 2 + 4 = 8 cm²

A third way is to imagine cutting off triangle C and moving it over to the other side to make a rectangle.

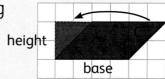

The area of the rectangle is 4 × 2 = 8 cm².

This gives us a formula for working out the area of any parallelogram:

Area of a parallelogram = base × height

$$A = bh$$

1 Find the areas of these parallelograms.

a

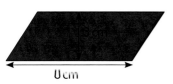

8 cm

b

5 cm

2 Find the areas of parallelograms with the following measurements.

    a base = 6 cm, height = 5 cm   **b** base = 10 cm, height = 3.8 cm

    c base = 3.5 cm, height = 8 cm   **d** base = 7 cm, height = 9 cm

Areas of compound shapes

You can already work out the area of a square and the area of a rectangle:

Area of a square = side × side

Area of a rectangle = length × width

A **compound shape** is made up of other shapes. You can work out its area by adding or subtracting the areas of the shapes it is made of.

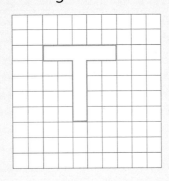 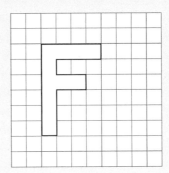

Count the squares to work out the area of each shape.

1 Work out the area of each unshaded shape by counting the centimetre squares (cm²).

a  **b**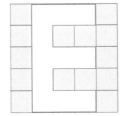

2 Calculate the area of each shape.
Divide the shapes into squares or rectangles to make it easier.

a **b** **c** **d**

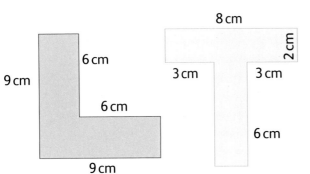 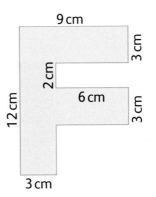 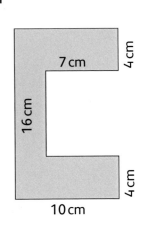

Surface area of 3-D shapes

Explain

To calculate the surface area of a 3-D shape:
- Count the faces.
- Calculate the surface area of each face.
- Add up the surface areas of the faces.

Remember these formulae:
- Area of a rectangle = length × width
- Area of a square = side × side
- Area of a triangle = $\frac{1}{2}$ (base × height)

1 Use what you know about area to calculate the surface areas of these solids.

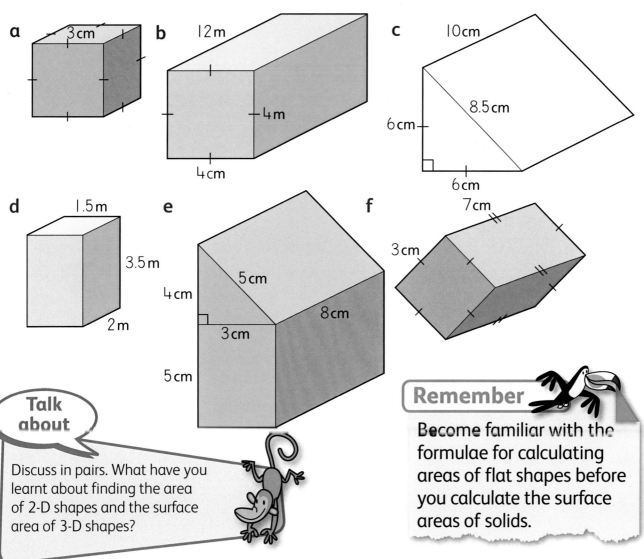

a 3 cm

b 12 m 4 m 4 cm

c 10 cm 8.5 cm 6 cm 6 cm

d 1.5 m 3.5 m 2 m

e 5 cm 4 cm 3 cm 8 cm 5 cm

f 7 cm 3 cm

Talk about

Discuss in pairs. What have you learnt about finding the area of 2-D shapes and the surface area of 3-D shapes?

Remember

Become familiar with the formulae for calculating areas of flat shapes before you calculate the surface areas of solids.

15 Volume

Unit solids

Solids have three dimensions: length, width and height. This is why we call them three-dimensional (3-D) objects. We can classify 3-D objects in different ways:

- whether or not they roll
- the number of faces
- whether they have flat or curved faces
- the number of vertices.

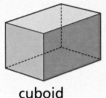

| cuboid | cube | cylinder | cone | triangular prism | square-based pyramid | triangle-based pyramid | sphere |

This cube has length, width and depth equal to 1 cm.

The **volume** of the solid is the amount of space it takes up. We express volume in cubic units, such as cubic centimetres (cm³).

This cube takes up 1 cm × 1 cm × 1 cm = 1 cm³.

1 Look at these shapes made out of 1 cm³ cubes.
Work out the total volume of each shape by adding up the number of cubes.

a   **b**   **c**  **d**

2 A chalk box has length 147 mm, width 72 mm and height 100 mm.
What is the volume of the chalk box in cm³?

Reasoning activity

What do you notice about the volumes of the two cuboids below? Can you think of any generalisations for your observations. How could you test your ideas?

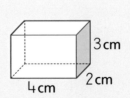
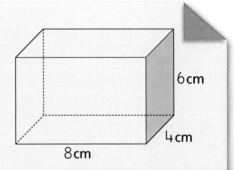

More about volume

Explain

The **volume** of a solid is the amount of space it occupies.

1 Use centimetre cubes to make these solids.
   Then find the volume of each in cubic centimetres.

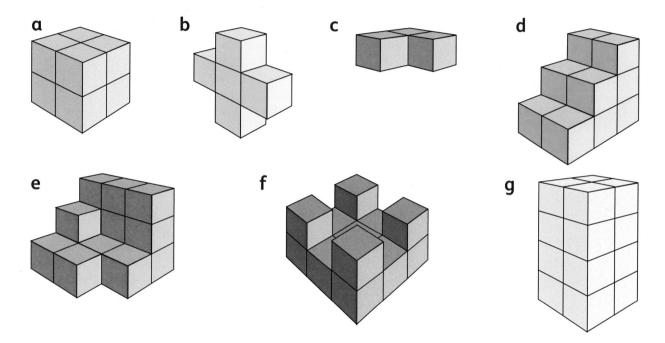

a   **b**   **c**   **d**

e   **f**   **g**

2 Draw diagrams to show these problems, and then work out the answers.
   You could also use cubes to help you.

   a In a box of milk, six tins can fit in one row, and the box can take four rows.
   How many tins can fit in one layer in the box?

   b If the box can hold three layers of tins, how many tins can the box hold?

   c A crate of sardines contains 100 tins. Four tins fit along the width of the crate
   and five tins fit along the length. How many layers of tins are in the crate?

   d A carton of soap powder holds two boxes along its height and four boxes
   along its width. There are 48 boxes in the carton.
   How many boxes fit along the length of the carton?

   e A toy box holds 36 building bricks. The bricks are packed in four layers, with
   three bricks along the length of the box. How many bricks fit along the width of
   the box?

Volume of a cuboid

We calculate the volume of a cube or cuboid using the following formula:

Volume = length × width × height

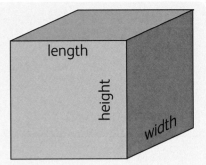

1 Find the volume of the following cubes.

a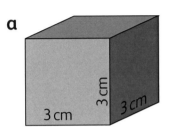

b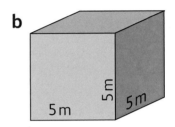

2 Find the volume of the following cuboids.

a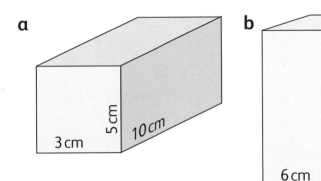

b

3 A rectangular box is 8 cm long, 6 cm wide and 3 cm high. What is the volume of the box?

4 The volume of a box is 162 cm³.
If the length is 9 cm and the width is 6 cm, what is the height of the box?

5 The volume of a tank is 2160 cm³.
The length is 15 cm.
If the width and the height are equal measurements, what is the width?

Try this

Does the formula $V = l × b × h$ always work when you try to find the volume of cuboids? Can you think of another method?

Exploring cuboids

Explain

What is the surface area of this cuboid?

We can work out the surface area of a cuboid by calculating the surface areas of its faces, and adding them together.

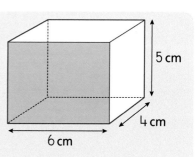

Two faces each have area 5 cm × 6 cm = 30 cm²   30 cm² × 2 = 60 cm²
Two faces each have area 5 cm × 4 cm = 20 cm²   20 cm² × 2 = 40 cm²
Two faces each have area 6 cm × 4 cm = 24 cm²   24 cm² × 2 = 48 cm²

60 cm² + 40 cm² + 48 cm² = 148 cm²

1 Calculate the surface areas of these shapes.

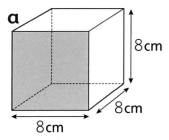
a 8 cm, 8 cm, 8 cm

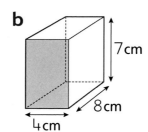
b 7 cm, 8 cm, 4 cm

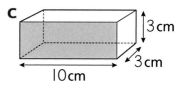
c 3 cm, 3 cm, 10 cm

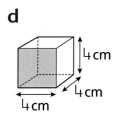
d 4 cm, 4 cm, 4 cm

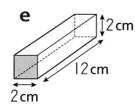
e 2 cm, 12 cm, 2 cm

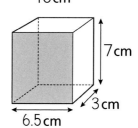
f 7 cm, 3 cm, 6.5 cm

Explain

The edges of a 3-D shape meet to form angles.

Where edges meet to form a square corner, they form an angle of 90°.

Edges may also meet to form angles which are smaller than 90° or greater than 90°.

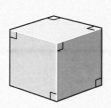

Can you see that each corner of this cube forms a 90° angle?

Each face also meets its adjacent face at an angle of 90°.

Talk about

Work in groups. Look at different packages and describe the angles formed by their faces. Explain four things to your partner about volume.

Symmetry

If a shape is folded in two parts and one part covers the other part exactly, the shape is **symmetrical**. The fold line is called a **line of symmetry**.

1 Trace these letters.

A B C D E F G H X Y

   a Which of them have lines of symmetry?

   b Draw in the lines of symmetry.

2 Trace these shapes.

   a How many lines of symmetry does each shape have?

   b Draw in the lines of symmetry.

   c Which shapes do not have any lines of symmetry?

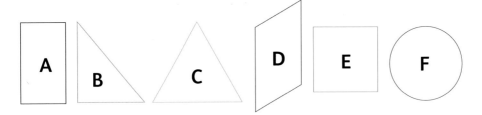

Reasoning activity

Use card strips and paper fasteners to join together to make different quadrilaterals.
Change the angles in each quadrilateral by twisting them.

a Do the shapes still have the same properties?

b Which shapes remain symmetrical or lose their lines of symmetry?

c What stays the same and what alters?

Test with other quadrilaterals and describe what happens when they are twisted.

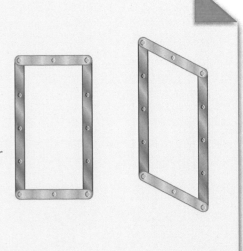

Congruence in plane shapes and solids

Explain

When two shapes can fit on top of each other exactly, they are called **congruent** shapes. That means that their corresponding sides and angles are equal.

 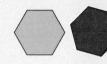 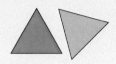

Each of these pairs of shapes are congruent.

Congruent solids are the same shape and size.

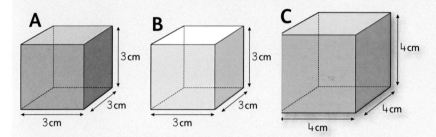

A and B are congruent because they are exactly the same size and shape.

C is similar to A and B because it is the same shape.

1 Identify which two shapes are congruent in each set.

Try this

Work with a partner. Each draw three different plane shapes. Exchange drawings. Draw three shapes that are congruent to your partner's shapes.

Remember

Note the difference between similar and congruent shapes. Similar shapes may be different sizes. When a shape is enlarged or reduced, the new shape is similar to the previous one.

Identify the pair of congruent solids in each set.

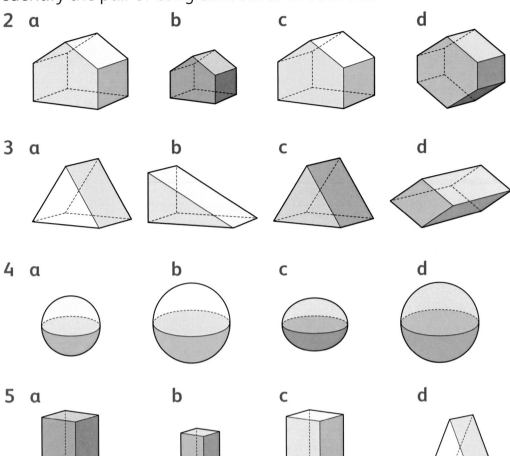

2 a   b   c   d

3 a   b   c   d

4 a   b   c   d

5 a   b   c   d

Work with a partner and make three pairs of congruent solids.

You will need:

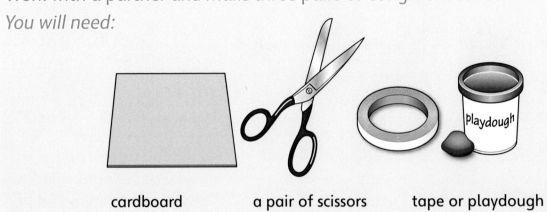

cardboard   a pair of scissors   tape or playdough

Which solids did you make? How did you make sure the shapes were congruent?

17 Coordinates and transformations

Simple coordinate systems

When you use a coordinates system, the horizontal and vertical axes are labelled *x* and *y*, and coordinate pairs are show in brackets in *x*, *y* order.

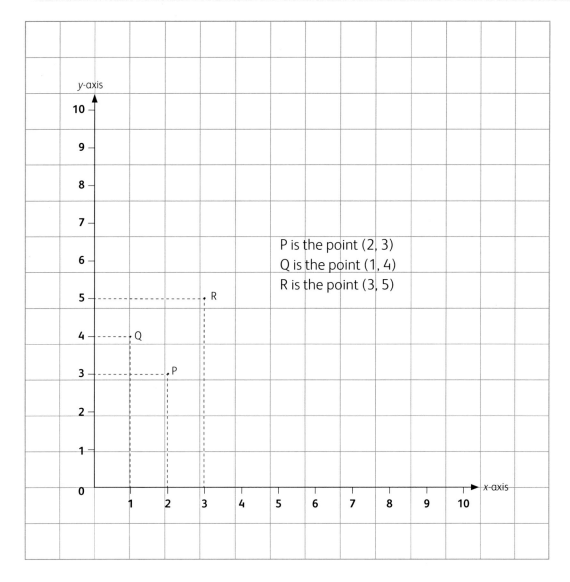

P is the point (2, 3)
Q is the point (1, 4)
R is the point (3, 5)

1 Use squared paper. Draw an *x*-axis labelled from 0 to 10, and a *y*-axis labelled from 0 to 10, as shown above.
On your grid, plot these points.

A (2, 5)   B (2, 3)   C (1, 4)   D (10, 6)

E (7, 9)   F (8, 2)   G (5, 8)   H (10, 10)

More coordinates

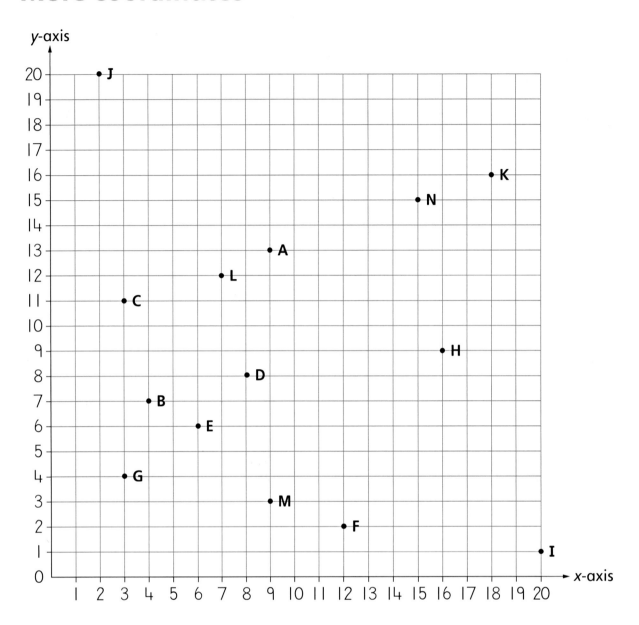

1 Give the coordinates of each point on the graph above.

2 a Draw *x*- and *y*-axes and label each axis from 0 to 10. Now plot the following points and join them in the order written below.

(1, 1), (1, 8), (5, 8), (5, 7), (2, 7), (2, 6), (4, 6), (4, 5), (2, 5), (2, 1), (1, 1)

b Name the shape you have drawn.

Transformations of plane shapes

A **transformation** is a change in the size, shape or position of a shape or object.
We can use translations to make patterns.

What would happen if we translated triangle XYZ 5 mm to the right, repeating this five times?

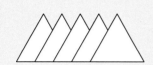

What would happen if we rotated triangle XYZ 30° about a point close to one of the vertices, repeating this 11 times?

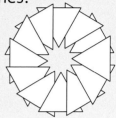

1 Work with a partner. Find a way to describe each of the transformations below.

a
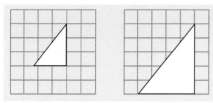

b
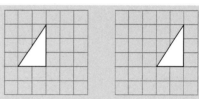

c
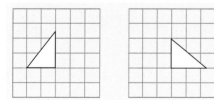

d
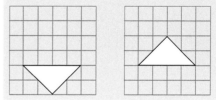

2 Choose a word from those below to describe each transformation:
- translation (slide)
- rotation (turn)
- reflection (flip)
- enlargement (making bigger)

Reasoning activity

Look at this triangle. Predict what patterns each of the following transformations would make. Test your predictions.

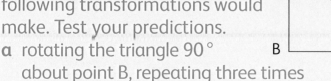

a rotating the triangle 90° about point B, repeating three times
b rotating the triangle 36° about point A, repeating nine times

Try this

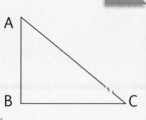

Draw and cut out your own triangle.
Use it to create five different shapes and three different patterns.

Transformations of 3-D shapes

Transformations are ways of changing the size or position of a shape. We can:

- translate (slide) shapes
- reflect (flip) shapes
- rotate (turn) shapes
- enlarge or reduce shapes.

To describe a transformation, we identify:

- how far it has moved
- the mirror line about which it has been reflected
- the angle by which it has been rotated
- the percentage or proportion by which it has been enlarged or reduced.

1 Discuss with a partner the type of transformation in each picture.

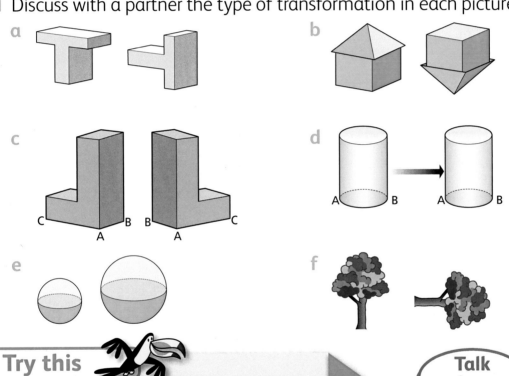

Try this

Play this game in small groups to explore transformations.

You will need: some 3-D objects, for example boxes, tins and dice, and a flat surface such as your desk. One of you gives an instruction to translate, flip or rotate the object in front of each player. Anyone who does the incorrect transformation is 'out'. The last one 'in' is the winner.

Talk about

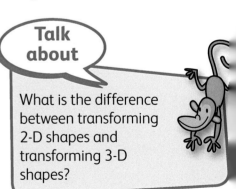

What is the difference between transforming 2-D shapes and transforming 3-D shapes?

18 Algebra, inequalities and variables

BOMDAS

Explain

When a calculation contains more than one operation, always do the operations in this order: **B**rackets, **O**f, **M**ultiplication, **D**ivision, **A**ddition, **S**ubtraction.
Why do you think we call this order BOMDAS?

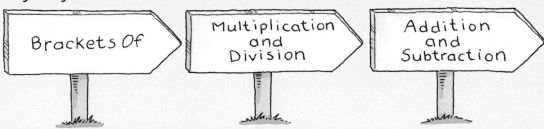

For example: $15 \times (48 - 12) + 8$
First work out the brackets: $48 - 12 = 36$
Then work out the multiplication: $15 \times 36 = 540$
Then work out the addition: $540 + 8 = 548$

Here is another example: $\frac{1}{2}$ of $30 + 5 - 6 \times 2 + (7 \times 4)$
First work out the brackets: $7 \times 4 = 28$
Then work out 'of' (division): $\frac{1}{2}$ of $30 = 15$
Then work out the multiplication: $6 \times 2 = 12$
Then do the addition and subtraction: $15 + 5 - 12 + 28 = 36$

1 Work out these without using a calculator.
   a $12 \times (25 + 11) - 18$ b $70 - 18 \times 3 + 25$
   c $21 - (16 - 8) \div 4$ d $100 \div \frac{1}{3}$ of (6×5)

2 Copy and complete these. Fill operation symbols to make each statement true.

   a $48 \bigcirc (3 \bigcirc 4) = 6 \bigcirc 6$ b $\frac{1}{2} \bigcirc 22 + 5 = 4 \bigcirc 4$

   c $90 - (\frac{1}{4} \bigcirc 40) = 100 \bigcirc 20$ d $8 \bigcirc 5 = \frac{1}{2} \bigcirc (100 \bigcirc 20)$

Working with inequalities

Explain

A mathematical **inequality** is a mathematical sentence which tells us about two values that are not equal to each other. For example:

$3 + 7 \neq 3 \times 2$ This tells us that the expressions on each side of the $\neq$ sign have unequal values. $\neq$ means 'is not equal to'.

We can also use $<$ and $>$ signs to describe an inequality. For example:

p is a whole number greater than 0, and $p < 5$.
Which values of p satisfy this inequality?
The $<$ sign tells us that p is less than 5.
Possible values of p: 1, 2, 3, 4

q is a whole number, and $0 < q \leqslant 7$
Which values of q satisfy this inequality?
The signs tell us that q is greater than 0 and that it is less than or equal to 7.
Possible values of q: 1, 2, 3, 4, 5, 6, 7

1 Write out these statements using symbols.
   a p is greater than two and less than or equal to ten
   b x is greater than or equal to one hundred
   c f is less than seven
   d m is greater than one-half and less than five

2 Write out these statements in words.
   a $3 \leqslant h \leqslant 11$ b $4 \geqslant i > 2$ c $9 < k \leqslant 50$

3 What are the values of p that would satisfy these inequalities, if p is always a whole number?
   a $13 + p < 16$ b $10 - p \geqslant 7$ c $p \leqslant 3$
   d $p < 4$ e $34 - p > 28$

4 Copy and complete these. Fill in $>$, $<$, $=$, $\geqslant$ or $\leqslant$ to make each statement true.
   a $3 + 6 \bigcirc 6 + 8$ b $7 + 13 \bigcirc 10 + 10$ c $63 \bigcirc 78$ d $3968 \bigcirc 4897$

   e $5 + p \bigcirc 13$ if p is a member of the set {0, 1, 2, 3, 4, 5, 6, 7, 8}

   f $18 - p \bigcirc 14$ if p is a member of the set {0, 1, 2, 3, 4}

   g $7 + p \bigcirc 10$ if p is a member of the set {0, 1, 2}

   h $14 - p \bigcirc 8$ if p is a any member of the set {1, 2, 3, 4, 5}

114

More inequalities

1 Write the possible values that satisfy each inequality. All of the letters represent whole numbers which are greater than 0.

   a t is a prime number. $t \leqslant 11$

   b y is an even number. $20 \geqslant y \geqslant 4$

   c k is an odd number. $k \leqslant 19$

   d q is a multiple of 3. $q < 20$

   e h is a multiple of 10. $50 < h \leqslant 100$

   f m is a factor of 24. $m \leqslant 8$

   g j is a factor of 50. $j \geqslant 10$

   h z is a prime number. $20 < z < 30$

2 Write out these statements using symbols.

   a Double 8 is less than 5 times p

   b q added to 25 is more than m multiplied by n

   c j is less than or equal to 10 and greater than 2

   d h is less than 100 and greater than or equal to 75

   e 3 times x is more than double y

   f 8 added to a is greater than or equal to 4 less than b

   g c divided by 5 is less than or equal to a half

   h f added to g is less than or equal to h less than j

3 What are the values of t that would satisfy these inequalities, if t is always a prime number?

   a $7 - t < 20$ b $16 - t \geqslant 9$ c $12 + t \leqslant 23$

   d $3 + (t \times t) < 30$ e $5t \leqslant 35$ f $8t < 40$

Talk about

Discuss and contrast an equation, which has expressions of equal value on each side, with an inequality, which has expressions of differing values on each side. Note that the ≠ sign simply tells us that two expressions are unequal. The < and > signs tell us more about the relationship between the expressions.

Using variables

A **variable** is a letter which we use to represent an unknown amount or number.
An **equation** is a number sentence which tells us that a pair of expressions are equal to each other.

For example, $2x = 6$ is an equation. x is the variable.
When we multiply variables, we don't use a multiplication sign. $2x$ means $2 \times x$.
We can use the equation to work out that $x = 3$.
Here are some more examples of working with variables.

1 If $a = 3$ and $p = 4$, find the value of the following expressions.

a $a + p$

$a + p = 3 + 4$
$= 7$

b p^3

$p^3 = 4^3$
$= 4 \times 4 \times 4$
$= 64$

c $3p$

$3p = 3 \times 4$
$= 12$

2 Work out the value of x in each equation.

a $\quad x + 3 = 10$

$x + 3 - 3 = 10 - 3$
$x = 7$

b $\quad \frac{x}{10} = 2$

$\frac{x}{10} \times \frac{10}{1} = 2 \times \frac{10}{1}$
$x = 20$

c $\quad 8x + 3 = 35$

$8x + 3 - 3 = 35 - 3$
$8x = 32$
$8x \div 8 = 32 \div 8$
$x = 4$

1 If $a = 4$ and $p = 5$, find the value of the following.

a $p - a$ **b** $4a - 2p$ **c** $5p$ **d** p^2 **e** $6a + 3p$

f p^a **g** a^p **h** $\frac{a}{p}$ **i** $\frac{3}{a} + \frac{2}{5}$

2 Work out the value of x in each equation.

a $4x + 6 = 30$ **b** $100 - 3x = 25$ **c** $12 + 2x = 42$

d $5x - 2 = 48$ **e** $10x + 20 = 110$ **f** $8 + 7x = 57$

Remember

Whatever you do to one side of an equation, you must do to the other side too!

Reasoning activity

Solve these problems. Write them out as equations to show your working.

Let: length = l width = w perimeter = p

a The length of a rectangular garden plot is twice its width. If the perimeter is 36 metres, what is the width of the garden?

b The length of a rectangular piece of land is 5 times its width. The perimeter is 48 m. What are the length and the width of the piece of land?

Solving problems using algebraic expressions and formulae

1 Mark's age is three times his sister's age.
If the total of their ages is 24 years, what is
Mark's age?

(Let his sister's age = a, then write the
number sentence to solve for a.)

2 The price of one kilogram of tomatoes
is half the price of one kilogram of potatoes.
If the total of their prices is $45.00, what is
the price of a kilogram of potatoes?

3 The distance from Kingston to
Constant Springs is twice the
distance from Kingston to
Half-Way-Tree. If the sum of the two
distances is 9 km, what is the distance
from Kingston to Half-Way-Tree?

4 A number y is divided by 6.
When 7 is added to this number,
the result is 10. What is y?

5 Three times a number is added to
four times the same number.
The result is 63. What is the number?

6 Shanara solved 8 more problems than Ariel. Together they solved
40 problems. How many problems did each girl solve?

7 Andrew and George divide $60 between the two of them.
If Andrew gets twice as much as George, how much does George get?

8 When 11 times a number is added to 26, the sum is 48. What is the number?

9 Six times a number p is subtracted from 80. The difference is 38.
What is the value of p?

10 Seven times a number q is added to 15. The sum is 260. What is the value of q?

11 Adrian's age is three times Jenna's age, and half of Max's age.
If Max is 90 years old, how old is Jenna?

12 Jessica has ten times as many game cards as Tina, and half as many as Jane.
The three girls have 372 cards altogether. Work out how many each girl has.

19 Money matters

Fractions and percentages

Problem solving involving money often requires calculating fractions and percentages.

It is easy to write a fraction with a denominator of 100 as a percentage because a percentage is like a fraction out of 100. For example:

$$\frac{20}{100} = 20\% \qquad \frac{11}{100} = 11\%$$

If the fraction is out of a power of 10, it is easy to convert it to a fraction out of 100. For example:

$$\frac{9}{10} \times \frac{10}{10} = \frac{90}{100}$$
$$= 90\%$$

To generate an equivalent fraction with a denominator of 100, we multiply both parts of the fraction by the same factor: For example, to express $\frac{3}{5}$ as a fraction with a denominator of 100:

$3 \times 20 = 60, 5 \times 20 = 100$

So $\frac{3}{5} = \frac{60}{100}$

1 Copy these and write the equivalent fraction with a denominator of 100.

   a $\frac{1}{2}$ **b** $\frac{3}{4}$ **c** $\frac{2}{5}$ **d** $\frac{7}{10}$ **e** $\frac{13}{20}$

   f $\frac{17}{25}$ **g** $\frac{30}{50}$ **h** $\frac{45}{50}$ **i** $\frac{16}{10}$

2 Write these fractions as percentages.

   a $\frac{22}{100}$ **b** $\frac{80}{100}$ **c** $\frac{24}{100}$ **d** $\frac{52}{100}$ **e** $\frac{7}{10}$

   f $\frac{4}{10}$ **g** $\frac{2}{10}$ **h** $\frac{6}{10}$ **i** $\frac{19}{20}$ **j** $\frac{15}{20}$

3 20 students are each asked to choose a snack – donuts or patties. 11 students choose patties and 6 choose donuts.

   a What percentage of the students choose donuts?

   b What percentage of the students choose patties?

   c What percentage choose neither patties nor donuts?

Financial institutions

Explain

Financial institutions are places where people can deposit their money and withdraw it safely as they need it. They include commercial banks, credit unions and building societies. As well as being safe places to keep your money, these institutions may also lend people money for large purchases such as houses, cars or property.

1 Choose the right words from the ones in brackets to complete sentence.

   a A bank or credit union is a type of (purchase, financial institution, building society).

   b Putting money into the bank is also called making a (purchase, loan, deposit).

   c Another name for borrowing money is taking out a (loan, withdrawal, deposit).

2 Use the following information to complete a copy of the bank deposit slip below.

- your name and address
- your signature and initials
- today's date
- account number: 32 451
- branch number: 23
- branch: Hagley Park
- amount: three $5000 notes, two $1000 notes, 20 $1 coins

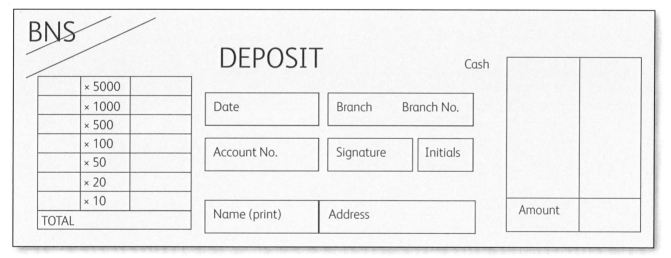

3 Mr Andrews wants to buy a car but he only has $500 000.00. This is a quarter of the price of the car. He borrows the remainder from the bank for three years, at a rate of 15%.

   a What is the cost of the car?

   b How much interest was paid each year?

   c Calculate the amount of interest to be paid in three years.

   d How much would Mr Andrews have saved if he bought the car at a cash price?

Money

When we write amounts of money, the decimal point is always between the dollars and the cents.

$9 807 241.15 is read as 'nine million, eight hundred and seven thousand, two hundred and forty-one dollars and fifteen cents'. Note that we do not write 'c' in dollar amounts.

1 Write the following amounts in words.

a
$215 600.50

b
$8 061 918.25

c
$1 000 754.00

2 Write the following amounts in figures.

a three million and two dollars

b three hundred and twenty-five thousand dollars and fifty cents

c two million twenty-five thousand dollars and seven cents

3 Five classes sold fudge to raise money for charity. This is how much they made in a day.

a Write the amounts in order from least to most.

b How much more did Class C collect than Class A?

c How much more did Class D collect than Class E?

A
$1550.00

B
$1280.00

C
$1840.00

D
$2320.00

E
$2280.00

4 Find the sum.

a $2123.00 + $5499.00

b $713.00 + $3482.00

c $23 455.00 + $344 877.00

d $41 219.00 + $1209.00

5 Find the difference.

a $5140.00 − $2387.00

b $3274.00 − $139.00

c $11 836.00 − $3490.00

d $356 985.00 − $34 564.00

Reasoning activity

The local animal shelter needs $46 000 to finish building a new set of kennels. Classes D and E decide to combine their amounts to raise this money for the animal shelter. If they raise the same amount each day how many days will it take to raise enough money?

Calculating interest

Explain

Edith wants to buy a car. The price of the car is $80 0000. She has only $300 000 to spend on the car, so she borrows $500 000.00 from the bank for three years. That means she will pay some money each month for three years, until she has paid it all back. The bank charges a fee for lending money. They calculate this fee as a percentage of the borrowed amount or principal. Edith's bank charges 2% per year. This is called **simple interest.**

> Simple interest (SI) = principal (P) × rate (R) × time (T)

a How much interest does Edith pay?

The principal is $500 000.

The rate is 2%.

The time is 3 years.

$500 000 × 2% × 3

= $500 000 × $\frac{2}{100}$ × 3

= $30 000

The simple interest is $30 000.

b What is Edith's monthly payment if she pays in equal amounts over the three years? (Round the answer to the nearest ten cents.)

$500 000 + $30 000 = $530 000

There are 12 months in a year. 12 × 3 = 36

$530 000 ÷ 36 = $14 722.20 per month.

1 Calculate the interest on each amount below. Copy and complete the table.

	Principal	Time	Rate	Interest
a	$6000	1 year	4%	
b	$30 000	1 year	5%	
c	$12 000	2 years	3%	
d	$4500	2 years	20%	
e	$18 000	3 years	40%	

Solving problems using simple interest formulae

1 Anthony borrowed $720 000.00 for five years at a rate of 15%.

  a How much simple interest must he pay?

  b Calculate his monthly payment, including interest, if he made equal payments each month for five years.

2 Mary borrowed $7000 for two years at an interest rate of 10%.

  a How much simple interest must she pay?

  b Calculate her monthly payment, including interest, if she makes equal payments each month for two years.

3 Tina wants to borrow $150 000 from the bank.
However, her bank has different rates for different time periods.

  • If you borrow money over one year, you pay 2% interest.

  • If you borrow over two years, you pay 3% interest.

  • If you borrow over five years, you pay 5% interest.

  a How much more interest will Tina pay over five years than if she borrows the money over two years?

  b Calculate Tina's monthly payment, including interest, if she borrows the money over two years and pays it back in equal monthly amounts.

  c Calculate Tina's monthly payment, including interest, if she borrows the money over five years and pays it back in equal monthly amounts.

  d Why do you think Tina might choose to borrow the money over five years?

4 Gloria wants to buy a house in Portmore that costs $2 000 000.00.
She decides to buy it through the National Housing Trust at a rate of 2% for 30 years.

  a How much interest will Gloria have paid after 20 years?

  b How much interest will she have paid by the end of 30 years?

  c How much interest would she pay on a monthly basis?

Try this

Each of the following words has another meaning that is different from its meaning in mathematics. Write two sentences for each word – one sentence showing its meaning in maths, and one sentence showing a different meaning. You may use a dictionary to help you.

  a principal   **b** interest   **c** rate

Calculating tax

Explain

Tax is an extra sum of money charged on goods and services. It gets paid to the government. In Jamaica, we pay tax on electricity, water, telephone calls and land. These are charged at different rates.

For example:

The tax on telephone calls is 16.5% and my telephone bill is $2400.00

a How much tax will I pay?

16.5% of $2400.00 $= \frac{165}{1000} \times \$2400$

$\qquad\qquad\qquad = \$396.00$

I will pay $396.00 tax.

b How much will I pay altogether for the bill, including tax?

$2400.00 + $396.00 = $2796.00

1 Calculate the tax charged on each of the following amounts, if the tax rate is 16.5%.

  a $3600.00   **b** $2800.00   **c** $4200.00

  d $8426.00   **e** $1204.00   **f** $5128.00

2 Calculate how much extra tax would be charged on each amount in Question 1 if the tax rate increased to 17%.

3 Mr Subawon imports refrigerators to Jamaica. A tax of 45% is charged on each refrigerator. What is the total price including tax of a refrigerator that costs:

  a $750 000.00   **b** $892 000.00   **c** $999 000.00?

4 Mrs York is a trader in exotic fish. For each fish she sells, she pays 26% tax to the government. If she sells six fish at $900.00 each, how much tax does she need to pay to the government?

5 Mr Smith buys a settee on hire purchase.
He pays $600 deposit and 12 equal monthly payments of $250.
The cash price of the settee is $2700.

  a What is the hire purchase price?

  b What percentage of the hire purchase price is the deposit?

Money problems

Go to a clothing store, or look at an advertisement in a newspaper.
Find prices for the following items:

jeans　　　pair of sneakers　cap　　　pair of shoes　T-shirt　　　shorts

Estimate, to the nearest dollar, the total cost for each of these shopping lists.

- two pairs of sneakers and a T-shirt
- three pairs of jeans and four pairs of shoes
- six caps and a pair of shorts

a Calculate the actual total for each list.

b Describe which notes and coins you could use to pay for each list without getting change.

c What is the smallest number of notes you could use to pay for each list, and how much change would you get?

Look at the menu for the Green Dragon Chinese Restaurant.

1 Jackie bought soup, six spring rolls and fried rice with vegetables.
  a What did her bill come to?
  b She paid with $2200.00. How much change did she get?

2 Simone and Daniel ordered three spring rolls, chicken chow mein, prawn noodles and four fortune cookies.
  a How much did their bill come to?
  b How much change would they get from $1500.00?

3 Imagine you are eating at the Green Dragon. Choose three items from the menu.
  a Estimate the total of your bill.
  b Now work out the exact total. How close were you?
  c Write down which notes and coins you would use to pay your bill exactly.

Soup $420
Spring rolls $500 for three
Lunch special $850 includes soup, meat, fried rice or chow mein
Lunch box special $935.00 includes meat with rice or chow mein
Fried rice with vegetables $750.00
Chicken chow mein $620.00
Prawn noodles $80.00
Fortune cookies $20.00 each

Talk about

How much would it cost you to eat at a restaurant close to your home?

More money problems

1 Look at the following prices for pants, T-shirts and sneakers:

Prices exclude tax

$900

$600

$2100

Paul buys three pairs of pants, four T-shirts and a pair of sneakers.
When he pays for his items, he is charged 16.5 % tax. Calculate the total cost, including tax, of:

a the pairs of pants　　**b** the T-shirts　　**c** the sneakers　　**d** all the items.

2 At a supermarket, Michael bought the following items:

- boxes of donuts at $120.00 each plus tax
- boxes of orange juice at $60.00 each plus tax
- 3 packs of soap at $70.00 each plus tax.

Tax is charged at 14.5 %.

a What is the total cost of all the items, including tax?

b How much more do the donuts cost than the soap (with tax)?

c Which costs more – the orange juice or the soap (with tax)?

3 A man bought six books for $400 each. The total cost, including tax, was $2760.00. Calculate the rate of tax charged on the books.

4 Tim bought five ice-creams. The price per ice-cream, before tax, was $200.00. He paid $1120.00 altogether in tax. Calculate the tax rate.

5 A store is selling shoes on sale. They reduce the price by 20 %. Hannah pays $1600 for a pair of shoes in the sale.
What was the original price of the pair of shoes?

6 A shop sells three boxes of ice-cream cones for a 30 % discount. The discounted price is $2100.00.

a What was the full price for the three boxes?

b What was the full price per box?

7 A bed set is on sale for 40 % less than full price. The price is now $2430.00. What was the price before the discount?

Discounts

Many shops offer **discounts** in percentages.
For example, Linda went shopping for shoes. The shop was offering a 25 % discount on the shoes she liked. The original price was $520.00. How much would Linda have to pay for the shoes?

25 % of $520 $= \frac{25}{100}$ of $520.00 or 0.25 × $520.00
= $130.00

Amount Linda would pay = $520.00 – $130.00 = $390.00

Supa-Shoe
Jamaica's discount shoe store!
Designer shoes now on sale!

Discounts up to 70 % on many styles!

Prices start from $485.00

Open 7 days a week.

1 Work out the sale price of each pair of shoes.

a Original price: $590.00 **b** Original price: $1275.00 **c** Original price: $695.00
Discount in sale: 35 %   Discount in sale: 30 %   Discount in sale: 15 %

d Original price: $845.00 **e** Original price:$499.00
Discount in sale: 42 %   Discount in sale: 25 %

2 Use your calculator to check your answers to Question 1.

3 For each pair of shoes in Question 1, find the difference between the original price and the sale price.

Profit and loss

Profit = selling price − cost price   **Loss** = cost price − selling price
If the selling price of an item is lower than the cost price (the amount the seller paid for it), the difference is called the loss, because the seller loses money. Sometimes a seller will sell things at a loss in order to get rid of unwanted stock.

1 Copy and complete this table.

	Item	Cost price	Selling price	Profit
a	giant fluffy bear		$129.99	$74.99
b	mini fluffy bear	$25.00	$49.99	
c	train set	$320.00		$439.99
d	bat and ball	$15.00	$29.99	
e	baby doll		$115.00	$65.00

2 Copy and complete this table. Work out whether each item was sold for a profit or a loss, and how much the profit or loss was.

	Cost price	Selling price	Profit or loss
a	$5.00	$8.00	
b	$10.00	$9.99	
c	$35.00	$45.99	
d	$215.75	$229.89	
e	$495.90	$485.99	

3 Lulu runs a shop in St Ann. She bought 16 bottles of apple jelly at $6 a bottle and sold ten of these bottles for $15 each. Since she needed to sell the apple jelly before the expiry date, she sold the rest of the bottles at a 50% discount.

   a What was the total cost price of the jelly?

   b How many bottles did Lulu discount?

   c What was the total selling price of the discounted bottles of jelly?

   d What was the total selling price of all the bottles of jelly?

   e Work out whether Lulu made a profit or a loss overall, and how much it was.

4 A shopkeeper pays $60 for a hand-sewn doll. He sells the dolls for $45.

   a What is the cost price of five dolls?   **b** What is the selling price of five dolls?

   c Calculate the loss he made.   **d** Find the percentage loss.

5 The cost price of a radio was $24 000.00. It was sold at a 12.5% profit. Find the selling price.

6 A rug was sold for $13 900.00 with a loss of 10%.

   a What was the cost price?   **b** Find the loss made.

Foreign exchange and hire purchase

Different countries use different kinds of money. These are called **currencies**. Some currencies used in the Caribbean are: East Caribbean dollar (EC$), Barbadian dollar (BD$), Jamaican dollar (J$), and United States dollar (US$).
For example:

US$1.00 = J$120.00

How much US currency do you need to buy J$120 000.00?

120000.00 ÷ 120.00 = 1000.00

You need US$1000.00

BDS$1.00 = EC$1.35

How much EC currency do you need to buy BDS$150.00?

150.00 × 1.35 = 202.50

You need EC$202.50

Hire purchase is a system which allows a buyer to pay for an item in regular instalments while having the use of the item immediately.

1 How much US currency do you need to buy:
   a J$470.00   **b** J$2000.00   **c** J$9000.76?

2 How much EC currency do you need to buy:
   a BDS$5.00   **b** BDS$26.00   **c** BDS$45.00?

3 US$1.00 = EC$2.65. Copy and complete these:
   a US$7.00 = EC$ _____   **b** US$120.00 = EC$ _____

Talk about

There are other currencies in use in the Caribbean. Research in pairs and find out their names.

Try this

Find out the exchange rate between Jamaican dollars and each of the following currencies.

a Japanese yen   **b** euro   **c** Australian dollar

4 Mr Joseph buys a refrigerator on hire purchase. He pays off the debt in 20 equal monthly payments. If the hire purchase price is $4500.00, how much does Mr Joseph pay each month?

5 A television set costs $9600.00 if you pay cash. Mrs Brown buys it on hire purchase. She pays a 25 % deposit and twelve equal monthly payments of $750.00 per month. Find:
   a the deposit paid   **b** the hire purchase price
   c the difference between the hire purchase price and the cash price.

Addition and subtraction problems

Reasoning activity

In these magic squares, all the lines of numbers (across, down and diagonally) add up to the same total.

4	3	8
	5	1
	7	6

16		12
	15	19
	14	

		212
213	215	217
218		

a Copy and complete the magic squares.

b In pairs, make up two magic squares of your own, using numbers greater than 5000. You can use a calculator. Leave four of the numbers missing, and exchange them with another pair. See who can work them out the fastest.

22 Smith Avenue $77 889

152 Long Street $192 559

5 Palm Road $272 995

96 High Street $95 999

15 Factory Road $65 779

85 Millionaire's Row $895 999

1 Between which two houses is there the greatest difference in price?

2 The house at 5 Palm Road was sold for less than the advertised price.
The seller accepted a price of $255 875.
How much less did she receive than the advertised price?

3 The prices above do not include tax.
This table shows what four buyers paid in total for their houses, including tax.
Work out how much tax was added on to each price.

House	Amount paid
96 High Street	$107 520
15 Factory Road	$73 675
152 Long Street	$219 517
85 Millionaire's Row	$1 021 438

Division and multiplication problems

1 Dina's roll of red ribbon is 3600 cm long. She uses it all to wrap 15 presents, cutting equal lengths of ribbon for each gift. How long is each piece of ribbon?

2 Steve is tying bows. He has a piece of blue cord 381 cm long, and he cuts it into 23 pieces of equal length with 13 cm left over. How long is the cord for each bow?

3 The Christmas balls arrived in a big box. The box had 48 rows, with 16 balls in a row.

   a How many balls were there altogether?

   b The shopkeeper packaged the balls in boxes of 14.
   How many boxes did she make, and how many balls were left over?

4 The shopkeeper received a parcel of gold stars. She divided the stars into packs of 12. She had enough stars to make 15 packs, and she had 3 stars left over.

   a How many stars were in the parcel?

   b Which number would we call the remainder?

5 Copy and complete these.

   a ___ × 38 = 3800   b ___ × 193 = 1930   c ___ × 96 = 960

   d 100 × ___ = 1000   e ___ ÷ 10 = 200   f ___ ÷ 100 = 12

   g 1000 ÷ ___ = 10   h 20 000 ÷ ___ = 200   i 41 × ___ = 41 000

Two-step problems

1 Lillian is going to Negril by road. She leaves Kingston at 05:40 and stops at Juicy Patties in Clarendon for breakfast at 07:50. She stays there for 25 minutes and then drives for a further 3 hours 15 minutes to Negril. How long did the whole journey take?

2 40 students in a Grade 6 class had a class party.
They could choose icicles or ice-cream. Two out of five students chose icicles.

  a How many in total chose ice-cream?

  b What was the difference between the number who chose icicles and the number who chose ice-cream?

3 What is the difference between the perimeters of the shapes?

4 What is the area of the blue portion?

5 The following timetable shows flights from Norman Manley International Airport. It shows departure and arrival times using 12-hour clock times and a.m and p.m.

Arrival city	Departure time	Arrival time
Miami	2:07 p.m.	5:00 p.m.
Panama City	3:02 p.m.	5:01 p.m.
Port of Spain	4:05 p.m.	7:45 p.m.
London	5:59 p.m.	8:50 a.m.
Montego Bay	6:00 p.m.	6:35 p.m.
Toronto	8:15 p.m.	1:30 a.m.

  a Joe arrived at the airport 1 hour 35 minutes before his departure to Panama City. The plane departed 40 minutes late.
How long was Joe waiting at the airport before departure?

  b Elsa arrived from Montego Bay for a connecting flight to Toronto. The flight was delayed by 1 hour 35 minutes.
How long did she wait for her flight at the airport?

21 Rate of travel

Distance, speed and time

When we travel, we often need to work out our speed to tell us how far we travel in a given time.

Average speed = $\frac{\text{Distance}}{\text{Time}}$

For example: Lisa cycled 8 kilometres in 2 hours. What was her average speed?

Speed = $\frac{8\,\text{km}}{2\,\text{hours}}$ = 4 km/h

We can use this rule to work out distance travelled or the time taken:

Distance = Average speed × Time

Time = $\frac{\text{Distance}}{\text{Average speed}}$

1 A car travels 240 km at an average speed of 50 km/h. How long does the trip take?

2 Mr Brown drove his car at an average speed of 80 km/h.
How many kilometres did he travel in:

   a 4 hours   **b** $5\frac{1}{2}$ hours   **c** $2\frac{1}{4}$ hours?

3 Copy and complete the table.

Average speed	Distance	Time
40 km/h	80 km	
36 km/h		$1\frac{1}{2}$ hours
	64 km	1 hour 20 minutes

Reasoning activity

These are the finishing times for a cycle race.
The distance of the race was 120 km. Find:

a Simone's average speed

b Jamie's average speed

c Ellen's average speed.

d Milly rode the race at an average speed of 50 km/h. How long did she take to finish?

Doogie takes the cup for the Smiley Lollipops Cycle Race!

Simone Doogie once again won the Smiley Lollipops Cycle Race. She finished the race in exactly $1\frac{1}{2}$ hours. Jamie Wallace took second place, finishing in 1 hour and 40 minutes, and Ellen Bryce took third place, finishing in 1 hour and 48 minutes.

Speed calculations

1 Evette Turner and Natoya Goule are two well-known long distance runners in Jamaica.

   a Natoya took 1 hour 30 minutes to run a 30 km race.
What was her average speed?

   b If Evette took 10 minutes longer than Natoya to complete the same race, at what average speed did she run?

2 Sam drove 680 km to meet his brother, at an average speed of 40 km/h. How long did his journey take?

3 Lisa, James and Maria all walk to school from their homes.
Each of them has an average walking speed of 4 km/h.

   a Lisa leaves home at 7:45 a.m. She lives 2 km away from the school. What time does she arrive at school?

   b James lives 3 km away from the school. He arrives at 8:00 a.m. What time does he leave home?

   c Maria leaves home at 8:00 a.m. and arrives at 8:15 a.m. What distance is it from her home to the school?

4 a A bus travels at an average speed of 50 km/h. It leaves the bus station at 12:00 and travels non-stop, arriving in Kingston at 14:30. How far has it travelled?

   b A second bus also has an average speed of 50 km/h. It makes the same journey but it stops three times, for 5 minutes each time. If this bus leaves the station at 13:00, what is the time when it arrives in Kingston?

Reasoning activity

Which animal is the fastest? Copy and complete the table.
You will need to work out how far each would run in 1 hour.
(However, most animals can only run at their top speeds for a short time.)

Animal	Distance (km)	Time (minutes)	Average distance covered in 1 hour	Average speed (km/h)
cat	12	15		
elephant	3	5		
giraffe	18	20		
kangaroo	1	1		
polar bear	5	10		

Measurement and road safety

Explain

When you cross a road, think carefully about:

- the width of the road
- the speed at which you can comfortably cross the road
- the speed of any oncoming vehicles.

Look at the diagram of two roads.

Road A

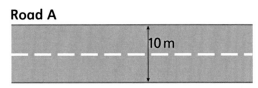

10 m

1 Which road is wider?

2 James crosses Road A. David crosses Road B. They start at the same time and walk at the same speed. Who crosses first? Why?

Road B

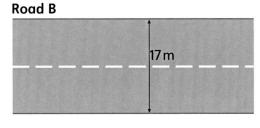

17 m

3 Imagine that a car was approaching 50 metres away from each boy, travelling at 60 km per hour.

   a Work out how long the car would take to reach the boy. (Hint: 60 km per hour = 1 km per minute)

   b Which car would get closer to hitting one of the boys – the car on Road A or the car on Road B?

4 Look at the paths these children used to cross the road:

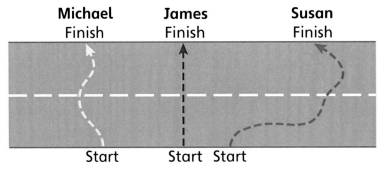

   a Whose path was the safest? Give a reason for your answer.

   b Whose path was the least safe? Give a reason for your answer.

5 Paul wants to cross a road. He can see two cars coming towards him. Car A is 25 metres away, and car B is about 400 m away.

   a Do you think he would be safe crossing before Car A passes?

   b Do you think he would be safe crossing before Car B passes?

   c What would be his safest option?

22 Circles

Circles

Explain

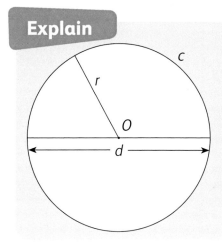

The outline of a **circle** is called the **circumference** (*c*). All points on the circumference are the same distance away from the **centre** (*O*). A **radius** (*r*) is any straight line drawn from the centre to the circumference.

A **diameter** (*d*) is a line that cuts a circle in half. The diameter must pass through the centre of the circle.

Work with a friend.

1 Identify each of the following parts on the circle above.

   a radius   b centre   c diameter   d circumference

2 a How many diameters does a circle have?

   b What is the relationship between the radius and the diameter?

3 Work on your own. Say whether each statement is true or false.

   a The diameter is the distance across the circle along any straight line that passes through the centre.

   b The radius is one-quarter of the diameter.

   c The plural of radius is radii.

   d A circle has only ten diameters.

   e All the points on the circumference are the same distance from the centre.

4 a Lines EO and OF are radii of this circle. EF is a diameter. Write down the letters for each other radius and diameter shown in the diagram.

   b Where is the centre of this circle?

5 a What fractions do the diameters AB and CD divide the circle into?

   b What fractions are created by the diameter EF?

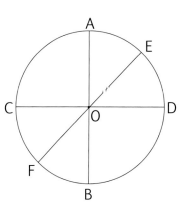

Circumference and diameter

Reasoning activity

Find a can which has a circular base.

a Measure the distance through the centre across the circular base.
What is this distance called?
Copy this and fill in your measurement.   D _____ = _____ cm

b Use a piece of string to measure the distance around the base of the can.
What is this distance called?
Copy this and fill in your measurement.   C _____ = _____ cm

c Now work out $\frac{circumference}{diameter}$. (We can also write this as 'circumference ÷ diameter')

d Repeat this with four other tins of different sizes.
Is there a relationship between the circumference and the diameter of a circle?
What is this relationship?

Explain

π is pi. This is a special number that we can represent as $\frac{22}{7}$ or 3.14.

$$\frac{circumference}{diameter} = π$$

$$\approx \frac{22}{7} \text{ or approximately } 3.14$$

circumference = π × diameter or 2 × π × radius

1 Calculate the circumference of each of the following circles. (Use π = 3.14)

a diameter = 5.5 cm
b = diameter = 8.2 cm
c radius = 7 cm
d = radius = 3 cm

2 Calculate the diameter of each of the following circles.

a radius = 9 cm
b = radius = 0.23 cm

3 Calculate the diameter of each of the following circles (Use π = $\frac{22}{7}$).

a circumference = 22 cm
b circumference = 88 km

4 Calculate the radius of each of the following circles (Use π = $\frac{22}{7}$).

a diameter = 10 km
b circumference = 66 cm

Talk about

Why is it not practical to work with the real value of π? (Hint: put 22 ÷ 7 into your calculator and see what happens.)

Measuring circles

1 a Use a piece of string to measure the circumference of each circle.

   b Use a ruler to measure the diameter of each circle.

   c What do you notice if you divide the circumference by the diameter for each circle?

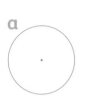
a

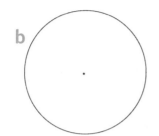
b

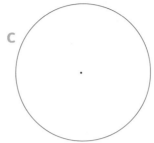
c

2 Calculate the circumference of the following circles. (Use $\pi = \frac{22}{7}$.)

a

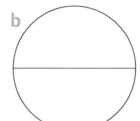
b

3 Use a pair of compasses to draw the following circles.

   a radius = 2 cm

   b diameter = 5 cm

   c radius = 3.5 cm

4 A cyclist rides around a circular field once. The radius of the field is 21 metres. How far does the cyclist ride if he goes around the field:

   a once   b three times?

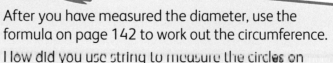

(Use $\pi = \frac{22}{7}$)

5 The diameter of a circular clock is 54 cm. How many centimetres does the minute hand travel in one hour? Use $\pi = 3.14$ to help you work this out.

Talk about

After you have measured the diameter, use the formula on page 142 to work out the circumference.

How did you use string to measure the circles on this page?

Is it more accurate to use string or to calculate using the formula if you need to find the circumference?

Finding the area of a circle

Explain

We can find the approximate area of a circle by placing it on a grid and counting the squares it covers.

This circle covers 5 whole squares and approximately 4 half squares.

$(5 \times 1) + (4 \times \frac{1}{2}) = 7$

The approximate area of the circle is 7 cm².

1 Find the approximate areas of these circles by counting the squares.

a 　b 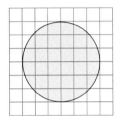　c 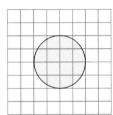　d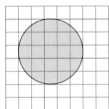

Explain

We can calculate the area of a circle using this formula:

Area of a circle = πr^2

For example:

a Find the area of a circle with radius 4 cm.

Area = $\pi \times r^2$

$\pi = 3.14$

Area = 3.14 × 4 × 4

= 50.24 cm²

b Find the area of a circle with radius 7 cm.

$\pi = \frac{22}{7}$

Area = $\frac{22}{7}$ × 7 × 7

= 154 cm²

2 Find the areas of the following circles.

a radius = 2 cm　　　　b radius = 3 cm　　　　c radius = 5 cm

3 At a primary school there is a circular playing field with a radius of 20 metres. What is the area of this field?

4 Derrick has a circular window with a radius of 1.2 m. He needs to replace the glass in the window, which is cracked. What is the area of the glass?

Looking at different kinds of angles

Explain

Angles inside a shape are called **interior** (meaning 'inside') angles.
Angles on the outside of a shape are called **exterior** angles.

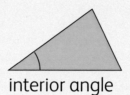

interior angle

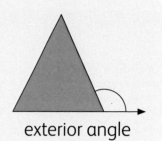

exterior angle

A **right** angle is equal to 90°.

An **acute** angle is smaller than a right angle (< 90°).

An **obtuse** angle is more than 90° and less than 180°.

A **straight line** is made up of two right angles which form a 180° angle.

A **reflex** angle is greater than 180° and less than 360°.

1 Classify these angles as acute, obtuse, right angle, straight or reflex.

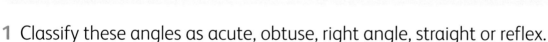

a   b   c   d   e

f   g   h   i

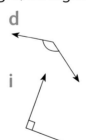
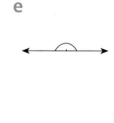

2 Count all the interior angles.

a   b

c   d

3 Count the number of angles in these diagrams at the point where the two lines meet.

a   b   c

Measuring angles using a protractor

Explain

You can measure angles using a **protractor**.

An angle is formed by two
line segments or rays that meet at a point.
Each ray or line segment forms an arm of
the angle. The point where the arms meet is
called the vertex.

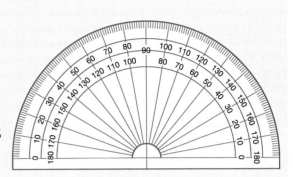

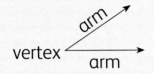

To measure an angle using a protractor:

- Place the centre of the protractor on the vertex of the angle.
- One ray of the angle must lie along the base line of the protractor.
- The other ray will fall on a degree greater than 0°.
- Read off the measurement where the second ray meets the scale of the
  protractor.

1 Estimate each angle, then use a protractor to find the exact measurement.

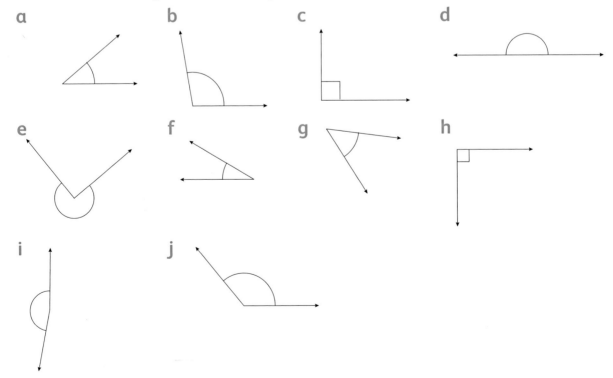

Drawing angles using a protractor

You can draw angles using a protractor. For example: Draw an angle of 140°.

Draw one ray.

Mark where you want the vertex to lie.

vertex

Place the protractor on the ray, with the centre point on the vertex.

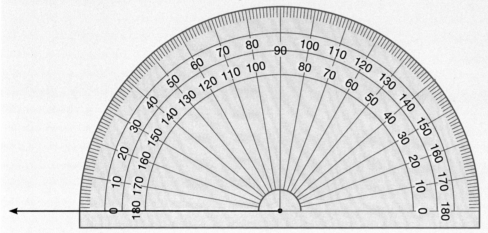

Mark the point where the protractor indicates 140° from the base line.

Remove the protractor and draw a straight line to join the vertex through the point.

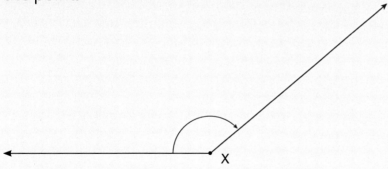

X

1 Draw the following angles:

  a 35°   **b** 60°

  c 90°   **d** 165°

  e 10°   **f** 200°

Remember

For reflex angles, you need to calculate the angle beyond the straight line, then add it to 180°.

24 Presenting data

Using bar graphs

Try this

Do a survey of your class to find out how the students travel to school. Use a tally chart to collect the information, and then draw a bar graph to present your findings. Use an appropriate scale on your graph, making sure that it is clear and easy to read.

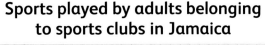

Sports played by adults belonging to sports clubs in Jamaica

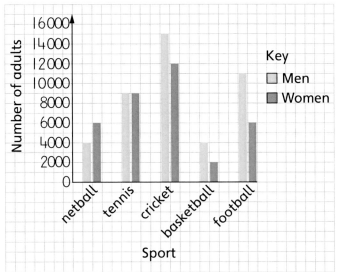

1 On this double bar chart, the numbers have been rounded to the nearest thousand.

   a Name the most popular game for men.

   b Name the most popular game for women.

   c What is the most popular sport?

   d Which sport is played by an equal number of men and women?

   e How many people play tennis altogether?

   f What is the total number of people who play cricket?

   g How many women play tennis, netball and cricket altogether?

2 **a** Arrange the sports in order from most to least popular among men.

   b Arrange the sports in order from most to least popular among women.

Making a graph about yourself

You will need: Graph paper, a ruler and a piece of string about 1 metre long.

What to do:

1 Ask a friend to measure your height in centimetres.

2 Measure the length of your foot.

3 Use the string to measure the distance around your waist.

4 Use the string to measure the distance around your neck.

5 Record your measurements in a table like this.

6 Make a graph to show the information in your table.
Let each large square on the graph paper represent 10 cm.

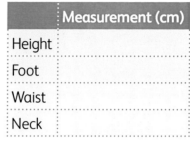

	Measurement (cm)
Height	
Foot	
Waist	
Neck	

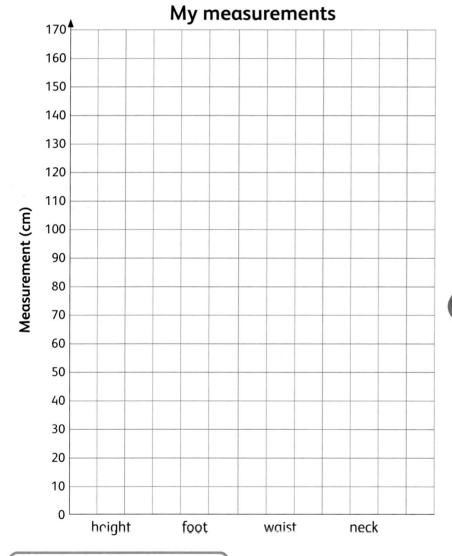

My measurements

Measurement (cm)

170, 160, 150, 140, 130, 120, 110, 100, 90, 80, 70, 60, 50, 40, 30, 20, 10, 0

height   foot   waist   neck

Talk about

In which jobs do you need to spend a lot of time measuring things in centimetres and millimetres? What kind of measuring instruments or equipment would you need for these jobs?

Reasoning activity

What conclusions can you make from your results?

Can you see any patterns or relationships?

Compare your graph with others. List some conjectures about your data and test them to see if they are generalisations you can make.

Solving problems with graphs

There were 20 students in a class. They received these scores in a mathematics test.

1 Copy and complete a table like this to show how many students received each score.

Score	Tally	Number of students
1		
2		

2 Use graph paper. Draw a bar graph to represent the information in the table.

3 a What percentage of the students received scores of 6?

   b What percentage of the students received scores above 6?

   c What was the average score?

   d Find the sum of the percentages in **a** and **b**.

4 *You will need:* A newspaper cutting showing football results like this one.

Arsenal	1	Manchester City	2
Crystal Palace	1	Nottingham Forest	2
Leeds United	0	Aston Villa	1
Liverpool	3	Tottenham Hotspur	0

a Make a table to show the numbers of teams who scored 0, 1, 2, 3 or more goals.

Goals scored	Tally	Number of teams
0	||	
1	|||	
2	||	
3	|	

b Draw a graph of your results. Label the x-axis 'number of goals', and the y-axis 'frequency'. For example, if 7 teams each scored 5 goals, the bar for 5 goals would extend to the frequency of 7. Don't forget to use a suitable scale for your axes.

c What number of goals was scored:

most frequently

least frequently?

Pie charts

1 This pie chart shows how Tina spends her pocket money every month.

a On what does Tina spend the least money?

b On what does Tina spend the most money?

c Does she spend more on fruit and biscuits together, or on the cinema?

d What is Tina's monthly pocket money?

2 This pie chart shows how Tina's mother spends her weekly wages.

a On what does Tina's mother spend the most money?

b On what does she spend the least?

c How much does she spend altogether on rent, clothing and food?

d What are Tina's mother's weekly wages?

e After paying for rent and electricity, how much money does Tina's mother have left for food, clothing and savings?

3 This pie chart shows how Martin spends his day. How many hours does Martin spend:

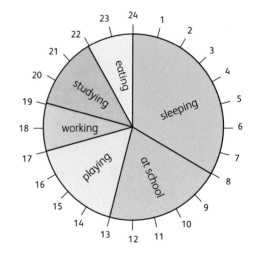

a sleeping   **b** eating

c playing   **d** studying

e at school   **f** working?

4 a Does Martin spend more time asleep or awake?

b How many hours does he spend awake?

c On which two activities does he spend the same amount of time?

Reasoning activity

a Draw a pie chart showing the way you spend your day. Is your day anything like Martin's?

b Compare your pie chart with someone else's. Are they similar?

c Write four questions based on your pie chart. Exchange questions with a friend and try to answer each other's questions.

145

More pie charts

1 The area of Guyana is 216 000 km². Use the information on the pie chart to copy and complete the table.

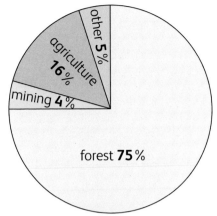

	Land usage	%	Area in km²
a	forest		
b	mining		
c	agriculture		
d	other		

2 This pie chart shows how Mrs Abraham intends to spend her salary in March.

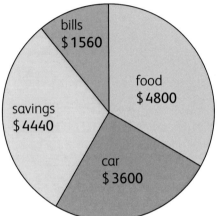

   a What is her salary?

   b What fraction of her salary is spent on food?

   c On which two sections combined will she spend about 44 % of her salary?

   d What fraction of her salary will she save?

3 The pie chart shows the favourite fruits of students in Grade 4.

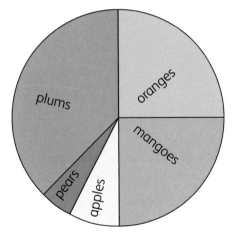

   a Which is the most popular fruit?

   b Which is the least popular fruit?

   c Which two fruits were chosen by an equal number of students?

   d There are 40 students in Grade 4.
   Only two students chose pears.
   What percentage of the students chose pears?

4 This pie chart shows the popularity of games in Tina's class.

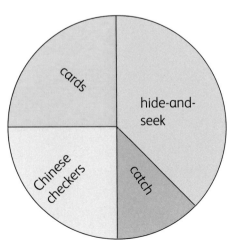

   a Which is the most popular game?

   b Which is the least popular game?

   c Which is more popular, cards or Chinese checkers?

Line graphs

1 This line graph shows the temperature in Ocho Rios at 12 noon over a period of 2 weeks.

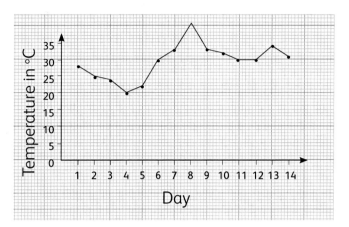

a Which day had the highest temperature at noon?

b Which day had the lowest temperature?

c What were these temperatures?

d During which season do you think this graph was drawn?

e Between which two consecutive days was there the greatest drop in temperature? What was the difference in temperature between these two days?

f Between which two consecutive days was there the greatest rise in temperature? What was the difference in temperature between these two days?

Try this

Using a thermometer, record the temperature in your classroom for a week. Draw a graph to show your findings.

2 The line graph below shows the population of the world over 250 years.

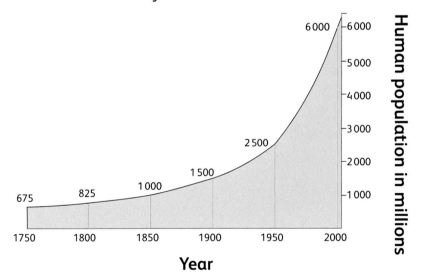

a When did the population start to grow at a much faster rate than before? How do you know?

b When did the world population reach 1 billion?

c After it had reached 1 billion, how many years did it take for the population to double?

d When did the world population reach 6 billion?

Different kinds of graphs

Here are some student test scores out of 100:

58	87	64	73	83	92	93	93	72	88
50	87	94	43	76	76	84	99	43	77
60	83	89	90	43	34	67	89	33	70

Let's look at some different ways of displaying this data.

A **stem-and-leaf plot** is a type of bar graph where the numbers form the graph. The 'stem' is made up of the tens digits and the 'leaves' are made up of the ones digits.

stem	leaves
3	4 3
4	3 3 3
5	8 0
6	4 0 7
7	3 2 6 6 7 0
8	7 3 7 4 3 9 9 8
9	2 3 3 4 9 0

You can easily see the distribution of the marks.

A **box-and-whisker plot** is another type of graph. First, arrange all the data in order from smallest to greatest. Then select the numbers that are approximately $\frac{1}{4}$, $\frac{1}{2}$ and $\frac{3}{4}$ of the way through the data. These values have been underlined below.

33	34	43	43	43	50	58	<u>60</u>	64	67
70	72	73	76	<u>76</u>	77	83	83	84	87
87	88	89	<u>89</u>	90	92	93	93	94	99

Finally, display the data like this:

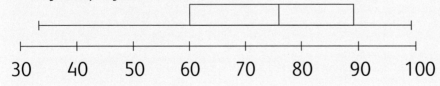

1 Draw a stem-and-leaf plot to show the following information.

Bunches of bananas picked on St Mary Banana Estate in 26 days								
63	42	39	84	63	98	63	65	65
33	48	49	68	73	74	79	53	64
49	81	83	92	94	90	87	64	

2 Answer the following questions about your stem-and-leaf plot.

  a Which stem has the most leaves?

  b Which stem has the fewest leaves?

  c Which stems have similar numbers of leaves?

  d What was the total amount for stem 50?

  e What does this graph tell us about the banana picking on St Mary Banana Estate?

3 Show the data from St Mary Banana Estate in a box-and-whisker plot. Select the numbers that are $\frac{1}{4}$, $\frac{1}{2}$ and $\frac{3}{4}$ through the data for your plot.

Try this

Measure the heights of all the students in your class in cm. Display the information in a stem-and-leaf plot.

Talk about

Discuss in pairs. What are the strengths and weaknesses of a stem-and-leaf plot?

Compare it to a box-and-whisker plot. Which do you find the most useful?

When would you be likely to use either of them when collecting and analysing data?

25 Probability

How likely?

We use **probability** to work out how likely or unlikely an event is. When we work with data, sometimes it is useful to think of all the possible results of an experiment so that we can work out which results are more likely than others.

1 Copy and complete these. Fill in 'more likely' or 'less likely'.
   a It is _____ to snow in Canada than in Mexico.
   b When you walk on the beach, you are _____ to see elephants than birds.
   c People who read a lot are _____ to be good at spelling.
   d Deserts are _____ to have a lot of rain than tropical rainforests are.
   e It is _____ to have a hurricane in August than in April in the Caribbean.
   f It is _____ that a plant will grow towards the light than away from the light.
   g You are _____ to see rain than sunshine in Jamaica in June.
2 Copy and complete these. Fill in 'impossible' or 'certain'.
   a It is _____ that the sun will rise tomorrow.
   b It is _____ that 100 years ago people could travel backwards in time.
   c It is _____ that if you leave an ice-cream in the sun, it will melt.
   d It is _____ for a human being to grow feathers on their head.
   e It is _____ that a butterfly will turn back into a caterpillar.
   f It is _____ that day follows night.
   g It is _____ for a pear tree to produce mangoes.
   h It is _____ that a coconut can fall upwards from a tree, instead of down to the ground.
   i It is _____ that this week will have ten days instead of seven.

Reasoning activity

a Work with a partner. Take turns to toss a coin. You should each try 20 times. Keep a note of how many times the coin lands heads up, and how many times the coin lands tails up.
b Find a way of representing your results in a chart or picture.
c Report your results to the class, and compare your results with other pairs. Discuss whether your results show that it is more or less likely that the coin will land heads up or tails up.

Equally likely outcomes

Explain

There are different ways of talking about probability. When we toss a coin, we can say that there is an **even chance** or a **1 in 2** chance of the coin landing heads up. Or we could say the probability is $\frac{1}{2}$ or 50%. When all the possible outcomes have an equal chance of happening, we say that the outcomes are **equally likely**. For example, when you throw a die, you are equally likely to throw a one or a six.

1 Jean puts four counters in a bag: one red, one blue, one green, one yellow. She takes the counters out of the bag at random, without looking. Choose the right answer from the ones in brackets to complete each statement.

 a When all four counters are in the bag, she has a (1 in 2, 1 in 3, 1 in 4) chance of taking a red counter out of the bag.

 b When all four counters are in the bag, she has a (20%, 30%, 35%, 25%) chance of taking a red counter out of the bag.

 c On her first try, Jean takes a green counter out of the bag. With the remaining three counters in the bag, what is the probability that she will take a red counter out next?

2 For each set of outcomes, write whether they are equally likely or not equally likely.

	Situation	Possible outcomes
a	A woman is pregnant.	A: The baby is a girl. B: The baby is a boy.
b	The days of the week are written on slips of paper and placed in a bag. Roy takes out one slip at random.	A: He takes out Monday. B: He takes out Tuesday, Wednesday, Thursday, Friday, Saturday or Sunday.
c	I throw a die.	A: The die lands on 6. B: The die lands on 1, 2, 3, 4, or 5.
d	I flip a coin.	A: The coin lands heads up. B: The coin lands tails up.
e	It has been sunny for 22 days.	A: Tomorrow will be sunny. B: Tomorrow will be rainy.

Expressing probability in different ways

Explain

We can express probability in different ways – as a ratio, a percentage or a fraction.

For example:

Peter has four coloured bottle lids in a bag – one white, one purple and 2 brown.

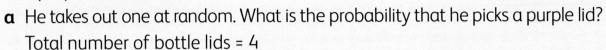

a He takes out one at random. What is the probability that he picks a purple lid?

Total number of bottle lids = 4

Total number of purple lids = 1

1 out of 4 = $\frac{1}{4}$

We can also express this as a percentage:

$\frac{1}{4} = \frac{25}{100} = 25\%$

b He takes out one at random. What is the probability that he picks a brown lid?

He has a 2 in 4 chance of taking out a brown lid.

2 out of 4 = $\frac{2}{4}$. This can cancel to $\frac{1}{2}$.

He has a 1 in 2 or 50% chance of taking out a brown lid.

1 There are the following balls in a bag:

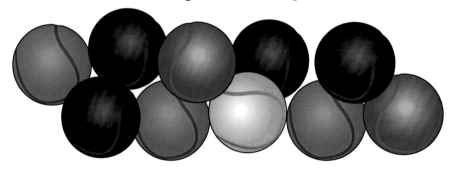

Copy and complete the table to show the ratio, fraction and percentage that express the likelihood of each of these possible outcomes.

Likelihood of picking	Ratio	Fraction	Percentage
Black			
Blue			
Green			
Orange			

More probability

1 There are 10 pairs of red socks and 10 pairs of yellow socks jumbled in a drawer.

a List all the possible outcomes of taking a single sock out of the drawer.

b If I take a single sock out of the drawer, without looking, what is the probability of getting a yellow sock?

c How many socks must I take out of the drawer to ensure I have a matching pair?

2 a Work with a partner. Take turns throwing a die. Take 20 turns each. Keep a note of your results in a tally chart.

b List all the possible outcomes of each throw. Write a few sentences explaining the probability of each outcome. Draw a probability scale to help you explain.

c What is the probability of throwing a 6?

d What is the probability of throwing an even number?

e What is the probability of throwing an odd number?

f What is the probability of throwing a 7?

In a pack of 52 playing cards, there are four suits: clubs, hearts, diamonds and spades. Clubs and spades are black, and diamonds and hearts are red. Each suit has 13 cards, as shown in the picture.

3 Margaret picks a card at random from a pack of 52 cards.
Draw up a table showing the probability that it is:

a a black card

b a king

c the ace of hearts

d a black jack

e not a spade

f a number card.

Try this

a Shuffle a pack of 52 cards and place them face down on a table. Pick up the top card and turn it over. Continue picking up cards until you pick up a diamond. Write down how many cards you had to turn over.

b Shuffle again and repeat the process. Repeat the process 30 times.

Probabilities practice

1 Copy and complete each statement. Fill in 'likely', 'unlikely', 'certain' or 'impossible'.

   a It is _____ that a restaurant would serve breakfast in the afternoon.

   b It is _____ that the sun will not rise tomorrow.

   c It is _____ that I will travel to the Moon tomorrow.

   d It is _____ that I will do some homework this week.

   e It is _____ that I will sleep tonight.

   f It is _____ that school will be cancelled for the months of January and February.

2 Choose the most appropriate answer to each question.

   a I take a number at random from a bag containing the numbers 1 to 10. What is the probability of taking out an odd number rather than an even number? (equally likely, 1 in 3, 1 in 10)

   b I throw a die. What is the probability that the die will land on a 5 rather than any other number? (equally likely, 1 in 5, 1 in 6)

   c I toss a coin. What is the probability that the coin will land heads up rather than tails up? (equally likely, 1 in 3, 100%)

3 Write the following probabilities as percentages.

   a 1 in 4   b 1 in 10   c $\frac{1}{2}$

4 Write the following probabilities as fractions in their simplest form.

   a 20%   b 8%   c 5%   d 40%

5 There are five oranges, three mangoes and two apples in a bag.

   a What percentage of the fruit is:

   • oranges   • apples   • mangoes?

   b What is the ratio of:

   • apples to total fruit   • oranges to total fruit   • mangoes to total fruit?

   c What fraction of the fruit is:

   • oranges   • apples   • mangoes?

6 I have a pack of 52 cards, shuffled so that they are mixed randomly. I pick a card at random from the pack.

   a What is the percentage chance of choosing a black card (clubs or spades)?

   b What is the percentage chance of choosing hearts?

   c What is the percentage chance of choosing a number between 1 and 5?

Assess and review 1

1 Write the correct symbol from the following list: $\{\,\}, \in, \cup, \cap, \longleftrightarrow, \subset, \varnothing$

   a union of sets   **b** equivalent sets   **c** member of

   d empty set   **e** intersection of sets

2 Draw a Venn diagram showing set A = {1, 2, 3, 4, 5} and set B = (4, 5, 6, 7}.

3 Draw a Venn diagram showing set X = (factors of 12} and set Y = (factors of 6}.

4 Name the members of the following sets.

   a {factors of 18} $\cap$ {multiples of 3 and 30}

   b {factors of 18} $\cup$ {multiples of 3 and 30}

5 List ten subsets of the set of factors of 18.

6 Are the following sets equivalent or not?

   a {letters in the word 'JAMAICA'} and {letters in the word 'TOBAGO'}

   b {even numbers greater than 0 and less than 10} and {dog, cat, bird, tree}

   c {multiples of 5 up to 15} and {C, A, T}

   d {triangle, circle, square, rectangle} and {pyramid, cube, sphere, cylinder}

7 Copy these and fill in the correct symbol ($\cup$, $\cap$ or $\subset$) in each circle.

   a {4, 8} $\bigcirc$ {factors of 40}

   b {5, 10, 15} $\bigcirc$ {whole numbers from 1 to 30}

   c {3, 5, 7, 11, 13} $\bigcirc$ {square numbers between 3 and 30}
       = {3, 4, 5, 7, 9, 11, 13, 16, 25}

   d {3, 5, 7, 11, 13} $\bigcirc$ {primes between 1 and 20}

   e {2, 4, 6, 8} $\bigcirc$ {primes between 1 and 10} = {2, 3, 4, 5, 6, 7, 8}

   f {odd numbers between 20 and 30} $\bigcirc$ {even numbers between 20 and 30}
       = {21, 22, 23, 24, 25, 26, 27, 28, 29}

   g {5} $\bigcirc$ {factors of 15}

Assess and review 2

Jimmy has a stand on the beach selling T-shirts.
He keeps a tally of how many T-shirts he sells each day.

Kind of T-shirt	Monday	Tuesday	Wednesday	Thursday	Friday	Saturday	Sunday
plain red			I	II	II		II
surfer	I		II	I	IIII	卌	卌 IIII
shells	II		卌		卌	III	I
plain blue	I			II	III		III
starfish	卌 I		III	I	卌 IIII	卌 卌	卌 卌 卌 II

I = 1 T-shirt   卌 = 5 T-shirts

1 a How many T-shirts did he sell altogether?

  b What kind of T-shirts was the most popular?

  c On which day did he sell the fewest T-shirts?

2 Draw a bar graph showing Jimmy's sales of each kind of T-shirt.

3 Draw a stem-and-leaf plot showing Jimmy's sales each day of the week.

4 a Calculate the mean number of T-shirts sold from Friday to Sunday.

  b Calculate the mean number of T-shirts sold between Monday and Friday.

5 Explain how you would use this information if you were Jimmy.

6 Collect three different kinds of graphs or charts from newspapers or magazines. For each piece of data, explain how the information has been represented, and why you think the researcher has chosen this way to represent the data.

Was this review helpful? How did it help?

Assess and review 3

1 Order each set of fractions from largest to smallest.

a $\frac{2}{5}$ $\frac{1}{3}$ $\frac{3}{4}$ $\frac{4}{5}$ $\frac{1}{2}$ **b** $\frac{1}{12}$ $\frac{3}{5}$ $\frac{1}{6}$ $\frac{2}{3}$ $\frac{1}{10}$ **c** $\frac{5}{6}$ $\frac{9}{10}$ $\frac{11}{12}$ $\frac{4}{5}$ $\frac{2}{3}$

2 Order each set of decimals from smallest to largest.

a 0.0045, 0.00045, 0.45, 0.045, 0.0405   **b** 0.099, 0.018, 0.3, 0.03, 0.23

c 0.21, 0.011, 0.08, 0.5, 0.22

3 Which of these has 8 in the tenths place? 85.4, 0.862, 80, 35.18, 875.2

Work out these. Give your answers as proper fractions or mixed numbers.

4 a $\frac{1}{4}+\frac{1}{5}$ **b** $\frac{1}{3}+\frac{11}{12}$ **c** $\frac{1}{7}+\frac{2}{3}$ **d** $\frac{4}{5}+\frac{1}{3}$

5 a $1\frac{2}{3}-\frac{3}{4}$ **b** $5\frac{1}{6}-2\frac{7}{8}$ **c** $6\frac{2}{8}-5\frac{1}{2}$ **d** $3\frac{7}{8}-1\frac{3}{4}$

6 a $2\frac{5}{8}\times1\frac{3}{7}$ **b** $1\frac{1}{9}\times7\frac{1}{5}$ **c** $2\frac{5}{7}\times8\frac{2}{5}$ **d** $6\frac{1}{2}\times1\frac{1}{5}$

7 a $4\frac{1}{2}\div3\frac{3}{5}$ **b** $1\frac{4}{9}\div\frac{3}{8}$ **c** $6\frac{2}{3}\div\frac{12}{25}$ **d** $2\frac{2}{5}\div2\frac{2}{3}$

8 Copy and complete these sequences.

a 4.05, 4.06, 4.07, ___, ___, ___   **b** 98.6, 98.7, 98.8, ___, ___, ___

c 0.10, 0.11, 0.12, ___, ___, ___   **d** 48.16, 48.17, 48.18, ___, ___, ___

9 Work out these.

a 9.3 − 6.8   **b** 13.43 + 0.5 + 4.26 + 3.2 + 36.99   **c** 11.5 − 7.9 + 5.1

10 Work out these.

a $2\frac{1}{2}+7\frac{3}{4}$ **b** $2\frac{1}{6}+1\frac{3}{4}+3\frac{2}{3}$ **c** $10\frac{7}{8}-4\frac{3}{8}$ **d** $8\frac{2}{3}-2\frac{5}{9}$

11 Copy and complete these.

a $\frac{1}{2}=\frac{\square}{12}=\frac{35}{\square}$ **b** $\frac{6}{8}=\frac{\square}{24}=\frac{3}{\square}$ **c** $\frac{5}{7}=\frac{\square}{21}=\frac{20}{\square}$ **d** $\frac{9}{10}=\frac{\square}{20}=\frac{81}{\square}$

12 Write each of these as a decimal.

a $\frac{8}{10}$ **b** $\frac{3}{100}$ **c** $2\frac{1}{10}$ **d** $1\frac{5}{100}$ **e** $\frac{2}{5}$ **f** $2\frac{1}{4}$

13 Work out these.

a 0.25 ÷ 0.05   **b** 0.125 ÷ 0.5   **c** 6.36 ÷ 0.3

14 A 3.6 metre length of ribbon is divided equally among four girls. What is the length of each ribbon?

15 David saved $520 in five days. How much did he save each day?

Assess and review 4

1. What does BOMDAS stand for?

2. Copy and complete these. Fill in operation symbols to make each statement true.

    a $(4 \bigcirc 5) \bigcirc 3 = \frac{1}{2}$ of 54   b $(9 - 3) \bigcirc 10 = 5 \bigcirc 12$

    c $50 - (\frac{1}{2}$ of 70$) = 45 \bigcirc 3$

3. James bought 5 pencils for x dollars and 5 erasers at twice the price of the pencils. The total cost of the items is $330.00. What is the cost of 1 eraser?

4. Four girls picked y oranges, and 3 boys picked 6 times as many. Together they picked a total of 840 oranges.

    a How many oranges did each boy pick?

    b How many oranges did each girl pick?

5. Sweets are sold at p cents, and chocolates for four times as much. Daniella spent $5 on sweets and chocolates. How much of it did she spend on:

    a sweets   b chocolates?

6. t is a prime number and $t < 9$. What values of t satisfy this inequality?

7. What are the values of m that would satisfy these inequalities, if m is always a whole number.

    a $m - 6 < 6$ b $m + 3 > 17$

8. Solve the following equations.

    a $6y - 80 = 40$ b $10x - 60 = 90$ c $\frac{x}{4} + 40 = 60$

9. When seven times a number is added to 14, the sum is 84. What is the number?

10. Pamella solved 8 more maths problems than Sharon. Together they solved 64 problems. How many did Pamella solve?

11. 6 boys picked y mangoes each, and 2 girls picked 3 times as many each. Together they picked a total of 636 mangoes. How many mangoes did each girl pick?

Assess and review 5

1 If BD$2.00 is equivalent to US$1.00, how many US dollars could I get for BD$7204.00?

2 Calculate the simple interest on $8000.00 for $6\frac{1}{2}$ years at a rate of 6%.

3 After two years the cost of a van decreases by 30%. Mrs Brown's van cost $1400 000 new. How much would she get for it if she sells it two years later?

4 Roy buys a school bag for $700.00 and a pair of shoes for $900.00. The tax is 15%. What is his total cost?

5 If J$87.00 is equivalent to US$1.00, how many US dollars would I get for J$13 920?

6 List two main purposes of financial institutions.

7 Peter buys a pair of pants for $400.00. He sells them for a 25% profit.

   a How much profit does he make?   **b** What is his selling price?

8 A TV set is priced at $56 000.00 before tax. The tax rate is 15%. Which of the following is the correct calculation for working out the total price of the TV set?

   a $56 000.00 × 15%   **b** $56 000.00 + 115%   **c** $56 000.00 + 85%

9 Write the following percentages as fractions.

   a 26%   **b** 75%   **c** $33\frac{1}{3}$%   **d** 65%

   e $12\frac{1}{2}$%   **f** 45%   **g** 55%

10 In a parking lot there are 20 cars. 8 cars are red, 7 are blue and 5 are green. What percentage of the cars are:

   a red   **b** blue   **c** green?

11 Copy and complete the table.

Percentage	Ratio	Fraction
40%	2:5	
75%		$\frac{3}{4}$
	7:10	
$33\frac{1}{3}$%		
50%		

12 Give an example of:

   a an empty set   **b** two intersecting sets.

13 The following statements are false. Explain why.

   a Equivalent sets have exactly the same elements.

   b You can count all the elements in an infinite set.

14 Give any subset of the set {names of students in our class}.

15 Draw a Venn diagram to show the universal set of even numbers up to 26 and the subset of prime numbers under 30.

16 A rectangular piece of land has a width of 12 m and a length of 18 m. Find:

   a its perimeter   **b** its area.

17 A square has a side of 65 cm. Find:

   a its perimeter   **b** its area.

18 Calculate the area of a triangle with a base of 4 cm and height of 6 cm.

19 Explain how it is possible to find the area of an irregular shape using grid squares.

20 Describe the events in the following sentences using the words 'certain', 'possible' or 'impossible'.

   a Saturday will come before Friday.

   b My favourite cricket team will win their next match.

   c The minute hand will move 360 degrees around the clock in the next hour.

   d I will wear blue jeans this weekend.

21 In a box there are 15 green toy cars and 5 red toy cars.

   a What percentage of the cars are red?

   b What percentage of the cars are green?

   c What is the ratio of green cars to red cars?

22 The letters of the word MATHEMATICS are written separately on slips of paper and put in a bag. A slip is drawn at random from the bag. Find the probability of drawing the following:

   a M   **b** E   **c** a vowel (any of the letters A, E, I O or U)   **d** T

23 A carpenter makes a table at a cost of $8000.00. He sells it at a profit of $1000.00. Calculate:

   a the selling price of the table   **b** the percentage profit he made.

Extended Project 1

The letter

Raymond received this surprise letter and cannot decide what to do. Help him choose a scheme and then write a letter to Great Aunt Sonia to explain why you have chosen it.

It would be a good idea to use a spreadsheet or draw a table of the amounts.

Keep the totals each year and a running total of the amounts to help you decide.

Dear Raymond,

Thank-you for your lovely birthday card, it is hard to believe that I am now 65 years old!

You will be pleased to know that I have decided to give you some of my money. I would like to give you an amount each year, starting now, or just a single amount. You can choose which of the following schemes you would like to use.

a) $20000 now, $18000 next year, $16000 the year after, and so on.
b) $200 now, $400 next year, $800 the year after, and so on.
c) $5000 now, $6000 next year, $7000 the year after, and so on.
d) $10000 each year
e) $80000 now and no more in the future

Of course, this scheme can only operate while I am alive. I look forward to hearing which scheme you choose, and why!

Best wishes,

Great Aunt Sonia

Running total each year					
Year	Scheme a	Scheme b	Scheme c	Scheme d	Scheme e
1	$20000	$200	$5000	$10000	$80000
2					
3					

Next step

- Can you see any patterns in the results to help work out any generalizations or formulae for the schemes?
  Test your formulae with other examples.
- Present the results as a line graph so that the different schemes can be compared.
- What if Raymond's Great Aunt was only 50 years old? Would it change your decision?

Extended Project 2

Washing machines

You are the head of a company that makes washing machines. You currently have four models.

The cheapest one, Model A, is the simplest with only two features, hot or cold wash and long or short spin.

How many different possible programs is that altogether?

	Hot wash	Cold wash
Long spin	✓	✓
Short spin	✓	✓

Investigate the different number of programs possible with your four washing machines.

Record your results so it is clearly explained. Is there a quick way of calculating the answer for any number of different programs?

MODEL A
- hot or cold wash
- long or short spin

MODEL B
- 3 temperatures: cold, warm, hot
- long or short spin

MODEL C
- 4 temperatures: 20°C, 40°C, 60°C, 80°C
- long or short spin

MODEL D
- 4 temperatures: 20°C, 40°C, 60°C, 80°C
- long or short spin
- fast or slow rinse

 Next step

A rival company boasts that their washing machine has 1000 different programs. Is this possible?

You now want to design two more washing machines models, with more features than the ones you currently sell. The top of the range must have 1000 possible programs.

Features could include these or any others you choose:

- pre-wash
- tumble-drying
- more temperatures
- timer

How many different programs are possible with your machines? What range and number of features can give exactly 1000 combinations?

You need to persuade a large hotel to buy your new washing machines. Design a leaflet advertising your two new models. Remember to highlight all the different possible programs.

Extended Project 3

What is the best insulator?

These line graphs show the results of an experiment to find out which materials are good insulators.

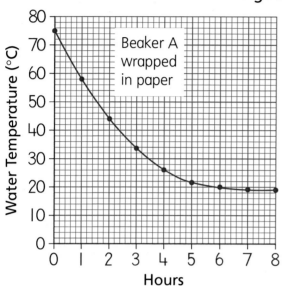

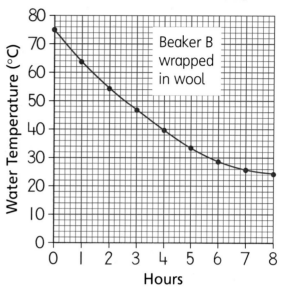

✱ What was the water temperature in Beaker A after four hours?

✱ How many hours did it take for Beaker B to reach 40°C?

✱ What was the difference in water temperature between Beaker A and Beaker B after 6 hours?

✱ Which material do you think is the best insulator – paper or wool?

This table shows the results using tin foil.

Water temp (°C)	75°	62°	54°	45°	38°	30°	26°	23°	21°
hours	0	1	2	3	4	5	6	7	8

Draw a line graph to show these results.

Compare the three graphs. Write 5 facts that you can find out from the graphs.

 Next step

A factory makes jackets for export. Work in a group to carry out your own science investigation into which material is the best and worst insulator for clothing.

- How can you make it a fair test? Think about the variables: size, time, volume.
- Record your results using tables and graphs.
- Which fabric would be best for a coat to keep you warm in a cold country?